Cambridge ICFE:

International Certificate in

Financial English

Workbook

First edition July 2008

ISBN 9780 7517 5493 3

British Library Cataloguing-in-Publication Data
A catalogue record for this book
is available from the British Library

Published by
BPP Learning Media Ltd
BPP House, Aldine Place
London W12 8AA

www.bpp.com/learningmedia

Printed by Thomson Litho, East Kilbride

We are grateful to Cambridge ESOL for
permission to reproduce extracts from the
Sample ICFE tests and the May 2007 ICFE tests.

Contents

Introduction

This is the first edition of BPP Learning Media's evolutionary new workbook for the Cambridge International Certificate in Financial English.

Cambridge ICFE has been devised jointly by Cambridge ESOL (English for Speakers of Other Languages) and the ACCA (Association of Chartered Certified Accounts). It has been designed as a global qualification to enable people for whom English is a second language to gain formal certification of their skills. This is of immeasurable assistance when working towards finance or accounting-related exams, or when aspiring to work for a global organisation.

This **BPP Learning Media workbook** has been written specifically for students who are working towards the Cambridge ICFE and is based upon the guidance provided by Cambridge ESOL. There is a section on each of the four components:

▶ Reading
▶ Writing
▶ Speaking
▶ Listening

Each section contains detailed analysis and explanation of the test requirements, worked illustrations and plenty of practice activities.

There is also a full mock test on each component, at the end of the book, for additional practice.

The **audio CDs** focus on the Speaking and Listening tests, providing realistic practice scenarios to familiarise students with the format of the tests.

If you have any comments about this workbook, please contact Pippa Riley at BPP Learning Media, e-mail pippariley@bpp.com

BPP Learning Media

July 2008

Introduction to the Cambridge ICFE

Background

The Cambridge International Certificate in Financial English has been devised jointly by Cambridge ESOL (English for Speakers of Other Languages), a department of the University of Cambridge, and ACCA (Association of Chartered Certified Accountants), the global body for professional accountants. The qualification has been developed to enable individuals and the organisations for which they work to have greater flexibility in an increasingly global financial world. English is the language of international business, and finance professionals now have access to unprecedented degrees of worldwide mobility. Possession of the Cambridge ICFE qualification means that they can demonstrate clearly that they have the requisite English language skills in the key arenas of communication: reading, writing, listening and speaking. Company human resources and training departments can now offer to their staff the opportunity to work towards a globally recognised qualification, providing evidence of a consistent standard of English. A successful performance in the ICFE test demonstrates the ability to use English effectively; it is not simply a reflection of good exam technique and the ability to pass exams.

Arrangements for taking the ICFE test

The Cambridge ICFE test is set twice a year, in May and November, at authorised Cambridge ESOL exam centres worldwide. For a list of centres currently offering ICFE, visit www.financialenglish.org. The website provides full contact details for all centres.

The tests of Reading, Writing and Listening will be scheduled to take place on the same day, consecutively. The test of Speaking may be organised over a longer period, as it takes place in very small groups. This will be arranged on an individual basis locally by the Cambridge ESOL centre.

The fee for taking the tests is set by the local Cambridge ESOL. You should contact your nearest centre in order to book to take the test. You will need to take all of the components at the same time.

The first test was set in May 2007.

The contents of the test

The four tests within the Cambridge ICFE are:

Test	Duration
Reading	1 hour 15 minutes
Writing	1 hour 15 minutes
Listening	Approximately 40 minutes
Speaking	Approximately 16 minutes

Each section within this Workbook will explain in detail the precise requirements of the test.

The texts and topics used within the tests are set in the context of finance and accountancy. We list below some of the areas that you might see:

▶ Financial reporting
▶ Company financial strategy
▶ Risk assessment and analysis
▶ Auditing
▶ Ethics and professionalism
▶ Accounting software packages
▶ Assets and company valuations
▶ Budgetary processes
▶ Corporate governance
▶ Cost and management accounting
▶ Environmental and sustainability issues
▶ Mergers and acquisitions
▶ Taxation (non-jurisdiction specific)

▶ Raising capital
▶ Insurance
▶ Banking
▶ Investment banking
▶ Professional practice
▶ The stock market
▶ Foreign exchange and currency
▶ Debt recovery and credit policy
▶ Bankruptcy and insolvency
▶ Forensic accounting
▶ Economic conditions and forecasts
▶ Pricing and purchasing

You do not need an encyclopaedic knowledge of all of these topics, although you are likely to have encountered most of them in preparation for accountancy or finance-related exams, or in the course of your working life. As you will see when working through the separate sections of the book, these topics tend to be quite generic in their coverage within the test. **Remember, the Cambridge ICFE intends to test your ability to communicate in English on finance-related topics, not your specific knowledge of finance and accounting.** The best possible way to prepare is to read and listen to as much finance-related material in English as you can, from as many different sources as you can find. Each section of this workbook suggests useful sources for preparation.

Marking and results

Each test carries a different total number of marks (for example Reading carries 70 marks and Listening carries 30). Each test is weighted so that each part contributes 25% of the total. The total mark available for the whole test is 200, after weighting.

There are three pass grades and two fail grades:

Pass	C1 Pass with Merit
	C1 Pass
	B2 Pass
Fail	Narrow fail
	Fail

The percentage of marks needed to attain each grade may vary a little from session to session, depending on the respective difficulties of the individual papers making up the overall test. Candidates do not need to attain a particular level in all four elements, as the final mark is based on the total score. Therefore if you perform badly in one part, you can compensate by scoring a very good mark in another part.

Results will be released approximately six weeks after the test, and certificates approximately four weeks after that. Results will be available online as soon as they become available. You can register for this at:

www.cambridgeesol-results.org/Members/Login.aspx

You will need the ID number and a password that your centre will give you when you register for the tests.

Candidates at each sitting will receive a comprehensive statement of results. This will indicate an overall estimate of their ability, based on performance in each of the four tests. This means that the four different skills tested will contribute equally to the candidate's overall competence. The statement of results will include a graphical profile indicating comparative areas of strength and/or weakness in the four skills, expressed as:

▶ Exceptional
▶ Good
▶ Borderline
▶ Weak

Successful candidates will receive a certificate from Cambridge ESOL.

If unsuccessful, candidates are required to take all four elements of the test again at a later sitting.

Varieties of English

The responses of candidates to tasks in the Cambridge ICFE are acceptable in the various forms of English which would enable candidates to function in the widest variety of international contexts. For example both British and American English are perfectly acceptable. However, candidates should try to remain consistent in the form of English that they use, and not, for example, change from American to British spelling in the middle of a task.

The material used in this Workbook and the ICFE tests themselves use authentic source material from English-speaking countries.

And finally……..

We at BPP Learning Media feel that you have taken a very positive step in deciding to take the Cambridge ICFE, and we wish you every success with this and your future career!

If you have any comments about this book, please contact Pippa Riley, Publishing Projects Director, at BPP Learning Media, by e-mailing pippariley@bpp.com

If you would like to learn more about the BPP Learning Media range of products for accountancy qualifications and business-related topics, please visit www.bpp.com/learningmedia

Reading

Contents of the Reading section

Introduction to Reading

Overview of the Reading Test

Test format

The paper consists of a range of finance-related texts and accompanying tasks. There are 6 Parts in all: Parts 1-3 focus on use of English while Parts 4-6 focus on Reading.

Timing

1 hour and 15 minutes in total.

Marks

Questions 1-36 (use of English tasks in Parts 1 to 3) carry 1 mark each. Questions 37-54 (reading tasks in Parts 4 to 6) carry 2 marks each. There are 72 marks available in total.

Answers

You must mark your answers clearly in pencil by filling in lozenges on the Answer Sheet (Parts 1,4, 5 and 6) or by writing a single word in capitals in boxes provided on the Answer Sheet (Parts 2 and 3). You should check the spelling of your answers to Parts 2 and 3, as incorrect spelling is penalized.

Summary of the Reading Test

Part	Task Type and Focus	Number of Questions/Marks	Text Type
1	Select a word to fill the gap Use of English: vocabulary/linking words and phrases	12 1-mark questions	2 short texts each containing 6 gaps and followed by 6 4-option multiple-choice items. You must choose the correct option to fill each gap and mark your selection on the Answer Sheet.
2	Think of a word to fill the gap Use of English: grammatical structure and vocabulary	12 1-mark questions	1 short text containing 12 gaps. You must think of the correct word to fill the gap and write it on the Answer Sheet.
3	Form a word to fill the gap Use of English: vocabulary (affixation and compounding)	12 1-mark questions	2 short texts, each containing 6 gaps. Each gap has a given base word. You must form an appropriate word to complete each gap, using the base word, and write it on the Answer Sheet.
4	Match summary statements to texts Reading: skimming for overall content (gist) and scanning for specific information (detail)	6 2-mark questions	1 text divided into 4 sections, or 4 related short texts, preceded by 6 summary statements. You must match each statement to 1 of the 4 texts, and mark your selection on the Answer Sheet.
5	Slot sentences back into text Reading: understanding structure, content, cohesion, coherence, global meaning, detailed meaning, argument	6 2-mark questions	1 text from which 6 sentences have been removed and placed in jumbled order after the text, along with 1 other sentence. You must decide from where in the text each sentence has been removed, and mark your selection on the Answer Sheet.
6	Multiple-choice questions Reading: for detail, gist, opinion, implication and referencing; understanding text and the opinions expressed, interpreting opinion and inference	6 2-mark questions	1 text followed by 6 4-option multiple-choice questions. You must choose the correct response for each question, and mark your selection on the Answer Sheet.

Do's & Don'ts in the Reading Test

DO	
✓	Read the instructions for each Part carefully and use any examples to help you.
✓	Think beforehand what order you would like to do the Parts in – for example, you may prefer to start with the longer Reading tasks (Parts 4, 5 and 6).
✓	Look at the words before and after the gaps in Parts 1, 2, 3 and 5.
✓	Check the spelling of your answers in Parts 2 and 3.
✓	Write your answers to Parts 2 and 3 clearly in capital letters.
✓	Leave yourself enough time to transfer your answers to the Answer Sheet.
✓	Allow enough time for reading Parts 5 and 6.

DON'T	
✗	Don't worry if you don't understand every word in a text – try to guess meaning from context.
✗	Don't leave any answers blank – you won't lose marks for wrong answers.
✗	Don't spend too long on any Part. Allocate your time according to the marks available. Remember the use of English tasks (Parts 1-3) are only worth 1 mark but the reading tasks (Parts 4-6) carry 2 marks each.
✗	Don't write more than one word for each Part 2 or Part 3 answer.
✗	Don't write in pen on the answer sheet – use pencil.

Preparation for the Reading Test

Do plenty of reading

The best preparation for the Reading paper is to engage with a substantial range of written English. You should therefore aim to do the following as you prepare for the test.

▶ Read extensively from authentic sources such as finance textbooks, journals, web pages and, if possible, examples of company reports and correspondence.

▶ Use the internet to access news and articles from the financial press of various English-speaking countries, as well as access to company websites which often include annual company reports.

Get help

You will find it useful to have as many sources of help as possible as you do your reading, and in the run-up to the test.

▶ Obtain a monolingual English dictionary to clarify the meaning of new words when reading for practice and to extend your vocabulary. You should make sure too that you are aware of contextual clues to help you guess unfamiliar vocabulary, as *you are NOT allowed a dictionary in the exam*.

▶ Obtain an English grammar book and use it if necessary when reading to improve your knowledge of language structure. *You are NOT allowed a grammar book in the exam*.

Become familiar with the test

Make sure you are aware:

▶ of the standard format of the Reading paper, the instructions on the front page of the question paper, and the rubrics for each Part of the test.

▶ how to indicate your answers on the separate Answer Sheet, so that you can do this quickly and accurately. Answers must be clearly marked by filling in lozenges on the Answer Sheet in pencil, or by writing a single word in capitals. You should check the spelling of your answers to Parts 2 and 3, as incorrect spelling is penalized.

Develop a strategy for the test

Decide the following points in advance of the test on the basis of practice using this Workbook.

▶ When you will transfer your answers on to the Answer Sheet – at the end of each Part, or once you have completed the whole paper? If you find the Practice Test in this Workbook time-pressured, for instance, it may be wiser to transfer answers after each Part, so you don't run out of time.

▶ How much time you will allocate to each Part. Each of the six Parts is worth an equal number of marks, but Parts that you find more difficult may require longer than those that you find easier.

▶ The order in which you will attempt the Parts. You may prefer to do the ones you find easier first.

Develop your reading ability (Parts 4-6)

You should be able to:

▶ understand a wide range of demanding finance-related texts including extracts from finance and accountancy text books and reference books, articles from financial journals, financial correspondence and other documents, company financial statements and annual reports and web pages (re-reading where necessary)

▶ quickly skim a text to identify its content and relevance in the context of international finance

▶ scan quickly through long and complex texts to locate relevant details

▶ read a text closely to identify finer points of detail including implied attitudes and opinions

▶ understand complex opinions and arguments

▶ read quickly enough to cope with a course of financial study at university level

Develop your reading strategies and skills

You should employ specific strategies and learned skills to demonstrate understanding of whole paragraphs or texts, not just sentences.

Parts 4-6 of the paper require you to have the following strategies and skills:

▶ Form an impression by skimming a text for overall content
▶ Scan for specific information and select relevant detail to perform a task
▶ Deduce meaning from context
▶ Read closely for detail

In addition specific Parts require specific strategies and skills:

▶ Part 4 (match summary statements to texts) requires you to retrieve specific information by skimming and scanning a text
▶ Part 5 (slot sentences back into text) requires you to read closely and demonstrate understanding of text as a whole and of how text structure operates
▶ Part 6 (multiple-choice questions) requires you to read closely and interpret text for inference and attitude

Most of the skills you need for reading are closely linked to using the right reading strategies. Experimenting with reading strategies in your wider reading can help to develop your general reading abilities and skills.

The following table should help guide you.

Reading STRATEGY	So you develop the following reading SKILLS:
Know why you are reading and what to look out for	▶ Selecting the right parts of the text to read ▶ Linking questions to specific parts of the text
Highlight, box or underline text and questions	▶ Relating text to questions, especially when referring back to check answers ▶ Excluding irrelevant information
Pace your close reading - slow down for difficult sections	▶ Ensuring that correct answers are not rejected just because they are more hidden in the text ▶ Understanding more difficult language
Mix skimming and scanning where appropriate	▶ Applying the right strategy to the right task
Make notes as you read	▶ Sifting and selecting the right information
Silently talk the message of the text back to yourself (at the end of each paragraph, for example)	▶ Summarizing, or forming overall impressions and understanding of the text as a whole
Make a note of and explore any confusion	▶ Deducing meaning from context
Check the style of the language (such as the use of linking words such as 'so', 'because', 'and', 'but' and 'or')	▶ Recognizing the text type through common patterns
Bring your own world knowledge to your reading	▶ Recognizing the text type and reading faster
Anticipate and predict	▶ Reading closely but faster; scanning or skimming more efficiently

Read faster

Being able to read relatively fast is an important skill when tackling the Reading exam. We saw above that if you develop the strategy of anticipating and predicting text you will improve your skill at reading fast. Here are a few other techniques you can try in preparation for the exam to improve your reading speed in the exam.

► Test whether you really are slow at reading – read something faster than seems comfortable and see how much you can remember. You may find that if you act as if you are a faster reader, you become one!

► Improve your concentration when reading by first reading some text for about 3 minutes and then adding a minute each time you attempt to read. You should find you can build up your ability to concentrate with practice.

► Keep your lips closed when reading, and don't 'speak' the words in your head as you are then only reading at talking pace, which is not very fast. Instead, try to interpret what you are reading, so that what you hear in your head is the message rather than the words.

► Use a ruler or pencil as a guide, moving it faster down the page to increase your reading speed.

► Concentrate on the 'beat' or rhythm that is in your head when you read, then work at making that beat faster.

► Look at 'sense groups' of two to three words rather than at every word.

► Ignore any words you don't know (you won't be able to do this in the exam, but it's a technique you can use in preparation to build up your reading speed).

► Keep reading - going back to earlier parts of the text slows you down and doesn't add that much to your understanding. If you skip over something, don't go back to it.

► Cover up the text that you are not reading to stop yourself jumping ahead or back.

► Focus on why you are reading

We shall now move on and consider each Part of the Reading Test in detail.

Part 1 introduction – selecting a word

What do I have to do?

Read 2 short texts and answer 6 questions to complete 6 gaps in each text, by selecting a word or phrase from four options A-D. Consider all the options carefully before deciding on your answer. Several may appear possible, but **only one option will be completely correct** in terms of meaning and grammar in that particular context.

How many questions/marks are there?

12 questions for 12 marks – 1 mark each (the Part is split into two 6-mark sections)

What texts are used?

Mainly extracts from reference books and financial textbooks, financial newspapers and journals, financial websites, company annual reports, research reports, correspondence and other documents.

What is being tested?

Vocabulary, linking words and phrases, fixed phrases, precision of meaning and shades of meaning

How should I prepare for the task?

▶   Read extensively from appropriate sources in order to build up a wide vocabulary.

▶   Pay attention to shades of meaning by watching out for usage of similar words, for words that often appear together (eg 'account for') and for words that are mostly exclusive (eg 'alive'/'dead').

▶   Practise linking words and phrases (this will also benefit your writing skills), for instance 'in addition', 'moreover' and 'nevertheless'.

Part 1 introductory exercises (selecting a word)

You should find these three introductory exercises helpful in relation to shades of meaning and linking words and phrases.

Part 1 introductory exercise 1

Adjectives describe nouns and are a very important element in vocabulary. In many contexts there are adjectives used which are mutually exclusive, for instance if a person was described as 'alive' they could not be described as 'dead'. Sometimes such opposites are formed by adding something to the original word (before - a prefix - or after - a suffix), and sometimes they are completely different words.

Complete the table below by identifying two opposites for each adjective. We have completed the first one for you.

Adjective	Opposite formed by adding something	Opposite as different word
Successful	Unsuccessful	Failed
Solvent		
Correct		
Standard		
Expensive		
Usual		

Part 1 introductory exercise 2

There are many words that mean one thing but when joined with another word develop a different 'shade' of meaning.

Match a word in column A with a word or phrase in column B that alters or extends the meaning of the A word. (Hint: Tick off each pair as you proceed.)

A	B
Float	Recovery
Settle	Risk
Depreciation	Governance
Assess	Exchange
Corporate	Capital
Debt	Accounting
Cost	Banking
Raising	On the stock market
Foreign	Charge
Investment	Debts

Part 1 introductory exercise 3

Especially in relation to understanding and interpreting text, you must appreciate how certain linking words/phrases (conjunctions) 'join up' two ideas.

Identify from the box below the linking word or phrase that should be used in column B to join up the ideas in columns A and C. (Hint: note that in one case you are looking for a word to link two separate sentences.)

Linking words/phrases

because	although	and	when	in addition	but	nevertheless	or

A	B Linking word or phrase	C
The auditor reports on the balance sheet		profit and loss account.
Some shareholders voiced severe misgivings.		The director was reappointed.
The directors are proceeding with the issue		they are taking the precaution of underwriting it.
The final tax charge has risen		of higher marginal rates in Europe.
The company must choose either the straight line		the reducing balance depreciation method.
The merger will proceed		the time is right.
Cash reserves are relatively high		the company's future is still uncertain.
Mr X has taken on the chairmanship of Y plc		to that of Z plc.

Part 1 Answers to introductory exercises

Answer to Part 1 introductory exercise 1

Adjective	Opposite formed by adding something	Opposite as different word
Successful	Unsuccessful	Failed
Solvent	Insolvent	Bankrupt
Correct	Incorrect	Wrong
Standard	Sub-standard/non-standard	Irregular
Expensive	Inexpensive	Cheap
Usual	Unusual	Rare

Answer to Part 1 introductory exercise 2

You probably found this exercise quite testing as there are a couple of words in the A column which match with more than one B column word. This highlights how important it is to be methodical when answering tasks. Tick off each pair that you are absolutely sure about, then consider very carefully the remaining possible pairings and reach a reasonable conclusion.

A	B
Float	On the stock market
Settle	Debts
Depreciation	Charge
Assess	Risk
Corporate	Governance
Debt	Recovery
Cost	Accounting
Raising	Capital
Foreign	Exchange
Investment	Banking

Answer to Part 1 introductory exercise 3

A	B Linking word or phrase	C
The auditor reports on the balance sheet	and	profit and loss account.
Some shareholders voiced severe misgivings.	Nevertheless	the director was reappointed.
The directors are proceeding with the issue	although	they are taking the precaution of underwriting it.
The final tax charge has risen	because	of higher marginal rates in Europe.
The company must choose either the straight line	or	the reducing balance depreciation method.
The merger will proceed	when	the time is right.
Cash reserves are relatively high	but	the company's future is still uncertain.
Mr X has taken on the chairmanship of Y plc	in addition	to that of Z plc.

The style and format of the six Parts of the Reading exam are very different. As it is quite a complicated exam it's important that you become properly acquainted with each Part separately before tackling a Practice Test as a whole. We recommend therefore that you:

▶ Skim through the following Part 1 Example, then the section on 'Getting started on the Part 1 Example'.

▶ Read through the section on 'How to approach the Part 1 Example' on page 20 before completing the Example and studying the answers on page 21, then

▶ Tackle the Part 1 Full Practice Questions on pages 22-25.

Part 1 Example (selecting a word)

► Read the following extract from an independent review report by an accountancy firm in a listed group's half-year review.
► Choose the best word or phrase to fill each gap from options A, B, C or D below.
► For each question 1 – 6, mark ONE letter (A, B, C or D) on your Answer Sheet.

There is an example task at the beginning (0).

EXTRACT: A REVIEW OF FINANCIAL INFORMATION

A review consists principally of making enquiries of Group management and (0) ....analytical procedures to the financial information and underlying financial data and, based thereon, (1) .... whether the disclosed accounting policies have been applied. A review (2) .... audit procedures such as tests of control and verification of assets, liabilities and transactions. It is substantially less in (3) .... than an audit and therefore provides a lower level of assurance. The report, including the conclusion, has been prepared for, and only for, the Group for the purpose of the Listing Rules of the Financial Services Authority, and for no other purpose. We do not, in producing this report, accept or (4) .... responsibility for any other purpose or to any other person to whom this report is shown, or into whose hands it may come (5) .... where this has been expressly agreed by our (6) .... consent in writing.

Example:

| 0 | **A** giving | **B** putting | **C** offering | **D** applying |

Answer:

| 0 | **A** [ ] | **B** [ ] | **C** [ ] | **D** [-] |

Options:

1	**A** regulating	**B** assessing	**C** perceiving	**D** realising
2	**A** excludes	**B** misses	**C** relegates	**D** eliminates
3	**A** capacity	**B** compass	**C** amount	**D** scope
4	**A** receive	**B** engage	**C** assume	**D** enlist
5	**A** except	**B** other	**C** apart	**D** besides
6	**A** forward	**B** prior	**C** preceding	**D** former

Indicate your answers here:

1	**A** [ ]	**B** [ ]	**C** [ ]	**D** [ ]
2	**A** [ ]	**B** [ ]	**C** [ ]	**D** [ ]
3	**A** [ ]	**B** [ ]	**C** [ ]	**D** [ ]
4	**A** [ ]	**B** [ ]	**C** [ ]	**D** [ ]
5	**A** [ ]	**B** [ ]	**C** [ ]	**D** [ ]
6	**A** [ ]	**B** [ ]	**C** [ ]	**D** [ ]

Getting started on the Part 1 Example

You need to think about the following points once you have skimmed through the text and options.

1 Where does the text come from?

The extract comes from a report on an independent review by an accountancy firm contained in a listed group's half-year review. Many companies make their financial statements available on the internet. You should make sure you familiarize yourself with authentic financial documents as they are often, as here, in fairly standard form.

2 What does the text deal with?

It deals with an accountant's independent review of the group's financial information as set out in its half-year review required by the Stock Exchange. It explains the purpose of the review report (not the half-year review itself) and how it relates to the Listing Rules of the Financial Services Authority. The financial English associated with financial authorities and regulations is an important area of vocabulary for you to know.

How to approach the Part 1 Example

1   Note the time as you commence the Task.

2   Read the brief description of where the extract comes from at the beginning, and check that the requirement ('choose the best word or phrase to fill each gap') is what you expect.

3   Skim read the entire text very briefly for its gist.

4   Start to read the text more carefully from the beginning, and when you get to Example Question 0 check that you agree with the answer given (this will boost your confidence).

5   As you get to each gap, look at the words before and after it and study the options offered. You should also consider the context. Choose the word that fits both grammatically and in terms of sense.

6   If you are in any doubt about how to fill a gap, try sounding in your head how each option would fit into the whole sentence.

7   On your Answer Sheet, for each of the 6 gaps make sure that you fill in just the lozenge related to your choice of option.

8   Note the time when you have completed your answers.

How long did it take you to complete the questions?

Probably about 5 minutes? It is difficult to specify how long you should spend on any one Part, but in the Reading exam as a rough guide you should aim to spend about 25-30 minutes on the first three Parts (36 marks), as the remaining three Parts require more reading time. This means you should spend no less than 4 minutes and no more than 5 minutes on a 6-mark Part such as this.

Don't worry if this Example took you longer than 5 minutes. Your speed will improve as you become familiar with the nature of the Parts and the approach you should take.

Study the correct answers to the Part 1 Example and make sure you understand the comments.

Answers to Part 1 Example

			Comments
0	**D**	applying	All the options for all three questions are verbs, which is what the context requires. This is a test of your knowledge of precise meaning. Note that different parts of speech may be covered across the six questions, including adjectives, verbs, nouns and adverbs.
1	**B**	assessing	
2	**A**	excludes	
3	**D**	scope	This tests your knowledge of the meaning and use of the noun 'scope'. The phrase 'less in scope' is used to compare the content of a review with that of an audit. **Phrases like this are commonly used in company financial reports and reporting standards documents and you should record the ones you come across in a vocabulary notebook.**
4	**C**	assume	This is also a test of the precise meaning of certain verbs.
5	**A**	except	The answer must be a single linking word that agrees with 'where'. This can only be 'except' since 'except where' makes sense while 'other where', 'apart where' and 'besides where' do not in this context. **You should always consider whether a particular grammatical pattern follows a certain verb, adjective or preposition.**
6	**B**	prior	This is a test of the precise meaning of certain adjectives (the word must agree with the following noun, 'consent'). The fixed phrase 'prior consent' is a useful one to know in the context of financial English.

Part 1 Full Practice Questions

Questions 1 – 6

▶ Read the following extract from an article about accounting ratios.

▶ Choose the best word to fill each gap from A, B, C or D below.

▶ For each question 1 – 6, mark ONE letter (A, B, C or D) on your Answer Sheet.

There is an example at the beginning (0).

EXTRACT: FINANCIAL STATEMENTS AND PROFITABILITY RATIOS

The financial statements of a business provide important information for people outside the business who do not (0) .... access to the internal accounts. For example, existing and (1) .... shareholders can see how much profit a business made, the value of its assets and the level of cash (2) .... Although these figures are useful, they do not mean a great deal by themselves. In order to (3) .... any real sense of the figures in the final accounts, they need to be properly analysed using accounting ratios and then (4) .... with either the previous year's ratios or against averages for the industry.

The profitability of a company is important and a key (5) .... of its success. In the profit and loss account the figures shown for gross profit and net profit mean very little by themselves. However, by (6) .... them as a percentage of sales they become much more useful. The figures can then be evaluated against those of previous years, or with those of similar companies.

Example:

0	**A** hold		**B** have		**C** grant		**D** keep

Answer:

0	**A** [ ]		**B** [-]		**C** [ ]		**D** [ ]

Options:

1	**A** eventual	**B** promising	**C** aspiring	**D** potential
2	**A** reserves	**B** stocks	**C** quantities	**D** stores
3	**A** reach	**B** find	**C** take	**D** make
4	**A** differentiated	**B** opposed	**C** compared	**D** balanced
5	**A** measure	**B** evidence	**C** mark	**D** proof
6	**A** indicating	**B** expressing	**C** outlining	**D** pronouncing

(Sample paper)

Indicate your answers here:

1	A [ ]	B [ ]	C [ ]	D [ ]
2	A [ ]	B [ ]	C [ ]	D [ ]
3	A [ ]	B [ ]	C [ ]	D [ ]
4	A [ ]	B [ ]	C [ ]	D [ ]
5	A [ ]	B [ ]	C [ ]	D [ ]
6	A [ ]	B [ ]	C [ ]	D [ ]

▶   Read the following article about the use of graphs in annual reports.

▶   Choose the best word to fill each gap from A, B, C or D below.

▶   For each question 7 – 12, mark ONE letter (A, B, C or D) on your answer sheet.

EXTRACT: GRAPHS IN ANNUAL REPORTS

Increasing attention is being paid to the visual (7) .... of corporate annual reports – the charts, photographs and graphs. Academics and practitioners alike (8) .... the immense power of good visuals in the communication process – a well-designed graph is worth a thousand words.

The existence of graphs of key financial (9) .... in corporate annual reports is a critical element of communication with stakeholders, especially non-experts. But graphs are not formally audited and there is the potential for graphs to be (10) .... so that they give too positive a picture of a company's fortunes.

A recent study has provided evidence that those responsible for annual reports consciously or unconsciously do indeed select graphical designs that tend to convey a more favourable impression than is (11) .... We, therefore, urge those who prepare reports to pay close attention to the basic principles of graph design and to seek clarity of meaning, before users lose (12) .... in the graphs displayed.

Options:

7	**A** components	**B** factors	**C** constituents	**D** facets
8	**A** conclude	**B** distinguish	**C** declare	**D** appreciate
9	**A** transformations	**B** variables	**C** permutations	**D** varieties
10	**A** manipulated	**B** influenced	**C** controlled	**D** operated
11	**A** entitled	**B** rated	**C** warranted	**D** earned
12	**A** assurance	**B** confidence	**C** belief	**D** conviction

(Sample paper)

Indicate your answers here:

1	**A** [ ]	**B** [ ]	**C** [ ]	**D** [ ]
2	**A** [ ]	**B** [ ]	**C** [ ]	**D** [ ]
3	**A** [ ]	**B** [ ]	**C** [ ]	**D** [ ]
4	**A** [ ]	**B** [ ]	**C** [ ]	**D** [ ]
5	**A** [ ]	**B** [ ]	**C** [ ]	**D** [ ]
6	**A** [ ]	**B** [ ]	**C** [ ]	**D** [ ]

Answers to Part 1 Full Practice Questions

			Comments
0	**B**	have	To 'have access to' is a fixed phrase. 'Grant access' is also a fixed phrase but is not relevant here.
1	**D**	potential	While 'aspiring' would make sense, 'potential shareholders' is the correct phrase.
2	**A**	reserves	Again 'cash reserves' is the appropriate phrase.
3	**D**	make	'Make sense of' is an important phrase related to understanding.
4	**C**	compared	The phrase 'compared with' works best in this context.
5	**A**	measure	'Evidence' and 'proof' here do not fit grammatically, while 'key measure' is a fixed phrase.
6	**B**	expressing	'To express as a percentage' is the correct phrase here.
7	**A**	components	While each word makes some sense, 'visual components' is the clearest expression here.
8	**D**	appreciate	None of the other options is completely appropriate.
9	**B**	variables	It is 'variables' that are plotted on the graph; none of the other options fits.
10	**A**	manipulated	The idea of manipulation is key to the sense of this sentence.
11	**C**	warranted	This is quite a fine shade of meaning.
12	**B**	confidence	The purpose of the information conveyed in graphs in this context is to give users 'confidence' in the company – so this is the appropriate word here.

Part 2 introduction – thinking of a word

What do I have to do?

Read one short text and complete 12 gaps in it by thinking of ONE word for each gap. Answers must be:

▶ grammatically correct both within the phrase and for the whole sentence

▶ appropriate to the meaning and context of the whole text: there may be more than one word which is acceptable for a gap, but you should supply one word only

▶ spelt correctly

How many questions/marks are there?

12 questions for 12 marks – 1 mark each

What texts are used?

Mainly extracts from reference books and financial textbooks, financial newspapers and journals, financial websites, company annual reports, research reports, correspondence and other documents.

What is being tested?

Grammar and phrase/sentence structure, with some vocabulary. In particular you are tested on:

▶ conjuctions such as 'and', 'but', 'or', 'because', 'of', 'in case', 'as soon as'

▶ prepositions such as 'at', 'throughout' and 'according to'

▶ pronouns such as 'I', 'them', 'his'

▶ quantifiers such as 'few', 'several', 'many' and 'all'

▶ auxiliary verbs such as 'be', 'do' and 'have' which are used to form tenses of other verbs

▶ modal verbs such as 'can', 'could', 'shall', 'should', 'may', 'might', 'will', 'would' and 'must' which are used with other verbs to express degrees of possibility and necessity

How should I prepare for the Task?

▶ Read extensively

▶ Be aware that some of the words which are gapped will correspond with the kinds of error that students make. Analysis and discussion of any regular problems you have with your writing may therefore be useful.

Part 2 introductory exercises (thinking of a word)

Part 2 introductory exercise 1

You should find these introductory exercises helpful in relation to prepositions, quantifiers and verbs.

Prepositions are words or phrases that link two items together. Generally they 'govern' the item that follows them, that is they indicate something about that item. For instance, in the sentence 'The company secured a listing on the stock market', the preposition 'on' governs 'the stock market' and links the first half of the sentence to the second. In financial English there may be more than one preposition that fits a context, but only one that forms an appropriate, frequently-used phrase (or 'fixed phrase').

Complete these sentences with a preposition from the box below them.

1 P and Co is the statutory auditor _____ T plc.

2 A final dividend was paid _____ the reporting period ending 31 December 20X0

3 The share price closed at $1.04, _____ 0.03c on the day's high of $1.07.

4 Strikes are endemic _____ the organization's European division.

5 H plc acquired a 40% stake _____ V plc today.

6 Motivation of staff is achieved _____ empowering them in every aspect of their jobs.

in respect of	by	in	of	down	throughout

Part 2 introductory exercise 2

Using the correct tense of verbs is critical to writing effective financial English, but being able to identify and interpret the subtleties of verb tenses is also an important element of reading.

In the extract below, choose the correct tense from the alternatives for each of the six numbered gaps in the following box. (Hint: you should read the entire extract first before attempting to identify what should fill the gaps.)

'Two years ago J plc, a major manufacturer, **1**_____ ready to launch Lemwal, a new product in the FMCG (fast-moving consumer goods) sector. Part of the preparation for this had been identification of the product's launch price, in which J plc's marketing director **2**_____ prices charged by retailers for similar products to end-consumers. However, he had omitted the vital wholesale market from his review entirely, and so the price he eventually **3**_____ was one on which wholesalers could not make a profit. Unfortunately at that time logistic factors related to the product's nationwide distribution meant that very few retailers **4**_____ take the product direct from J plc. Once the error **5**_____ recognised a new price was set and the supply chain was successfully formed, but the delay allowed a rival product to take market share and the product **6**_____ within six months.'

1	is/was
2	had reviewed/has reviewed
3	was setting/set
4	could/can
5	has been/was
6	failed/fails

Part 2 introductory exercise 3

Texts may sometimes be indefinite in relation to numbers and quantities, using 'quantifiers' to express relative or approximate rather than absolute or exact amounts.

In the following sentences, use the context to choose the appropriate quantifier from the alternatives for each gap. (Hint: you will find it best to test out each alternative in the sentence.)

1   In relation to the rights issue, the directors found that there were so **many/few** takers it had to be withdrawn.

2   The manager contended that **a few/a little** more effort would reap huge returns.

3   There were **several/enough** responses to the circularisation to allow the auditors to reach a conclusion on debt recoverability.

4   The successful sales team returned from their trip amid **many/much** celebration.

5   For a company with 50 shareholders holding one share each, votes in favour by 26 shareholders will form an effective **minority/majorit**y.

6   To meet their commitment to transparency, insurance companies try very hard to ensure that the terms and conditions of their contracts are understandable by **someone/everyone**.

Part 2 Answers to introductory exercises

Answers to Part 2 introductory exercise 1

1 P and Co is the statutory auditor of T plc.
2 A final dividend was paid in respect of the reporting period ending 31 December 20X0. *(This could also have been 'in'.)*
3 The share price closed at $1.04, down 0.03c on the day's high of $1.07.
4 Strikes are endemic throughout the organisation's European division. *(This could also have been 'in'.)*
5 H plc acquired a 40% stake in V plc today.
6 Motivation of staff is achieved by empowering them in every aspect of their jobs.

Answers to Part 2 introductory exercise 2

'Two years ago J plc, a major manufacturer, was ready to launch Lemwal, a new product in the FMCG (fast-moving consumer goods) sector. Part of the preparation for this had been identification of the product's launch price, in which J plc's marketing director had reviewed prices charged by retailers for similar products to end-consumers. However, he had omitted the vital wholesale market from his review entirely, and so the price he eventually set was one on which wholesalers could not make a profit. Unfortunately at that time logistic factors related to the product's nationwide distribution meant that very few retailers could take the product direct from J plc. Once the error was recognised a new price was set and the supply chain was successfully formed, but the delay allowed a rival product to take market share and the product failed within six months.'

Answers to Part 2 introductory exercise 3

1 In relation to the rights issue, the directors found that there were so few takers it had to be withdrawn.
2 The manager contended that a little more effort would reap huge returns.
3 There were enough responses to the circularisation to allow the auditors to reach a conclusion on debt recoverability.
4 The successful sales team returned from their trip amid much celebration.
5 For a company with 50 shareholders holding one share each, votes in favour by 26 shareholders will form an effective majority.
6 To meet their commitment to transparency, insurance companies try very hard to ensure that the terms and conditions of their contracts are understandable by everyone.

The style and format of the six Parts of the Reading test are very different. As it is quite a complicated test it's important that you become properly acquainted with each Part separately before tackling a Practice Test as a whole. We recommend therefore that you:

▶ Skim through the following Part 2 Example, then the section on 'Getting started on the Part 2 Example'.

▶ Read through the section on 'How to approach the Part 2 Example' on page 34 before completing the Part 2 Example and studying the answers on page 35, then

▶ Tackle the Part 2 Full Practice Questions on page 36-37.

Part 2 Example (thinking of a word)

▶ Read the following extract from a website article about evaluating company performance.

▶ Identify the best word to fill each gap.

▶ For each question 13 – 24, write ONE word in CAPITAL LETTERS on your Answer Sheet. Answers of more than one word will be marked wrong, even if they include the correct answer.

There is an example task at the beginning (0).

EXTRACT: EVALUATING COMPANY PERFORMANCE

It is clear that (0) ……….. is a need for companies in both the public and private sectors to develop appropriate performance measures. Setting performance targets and then evaluating achievements against these targets should provide a basis (13) ……….. improved management. It is important that these measures are not concerned simply (14) ……….. financial issues.

However, many difficulties will confront anyone (15) ……….. is tasked with developing a system aimed (16) ……….. setting up such targets. For example, the way in (17) ……….. objectives are set can present serious problems. In many cases, objectives are (18) ……….. vaguely drafted that useful performance measures can rarely (19) ……….. developed. Also, there is the difficulty of measuring quality, where the danger is that quantity rather (20) ……….. quality is emphasised, because, in almost (21) ……….. cases, quantity is easier to evaluate. Therefore, we get a somewhat distorted picture (22) ……….. easily measurable aspects of performance take precedence over those that are more difficult to measure.

(23) ……….. the importance of evaluating performance is recognised, the difficulties involved should not be overlooked. An awareness of these difficulties and an understanding of their possible impact should, however, lead (24) ……….. the development of more effective and better balanced systems.

Example answer:

0	T	H	E	R	E																

Indicate your answers here in CAPITAL LETTERS:

13																				
14																				
15																				
16																				
17																				
18																				
19																				
20																				
21																				
22																				
23																				
24																				

Getting started on the Part 2 Example

You need to think about the following points once you have skimmed through the text.

1 Where does the text come from?

It is an extract from a website article of unknown authorship and purpose.

2 What does the text deal with?

It deals with issues relating to the development of appropriate company performance measures. Cost and management accounting is a key finance-related area, so you should make sure you are familiar with the vocabulary contained in this extract.

How to approach the Part 2 Example

1   Note the time as you commence.

2   Read the brief description of where the extract comes from at the beginning, and check that the requirement ('identify the best word to fill each gap') is what you expect.

3   Skim read the entire text very briefly to get its gist.

4   Start to read the text more carefully from the beginning, and when you get to Example Question 0 check that you agree with the answer given (this will boost your confidence)

5   As you get to each gap, look at the words before and after it. The gaps can be filled by referring just to the immediate phrase or sentence.

      a   Circle the word or words in the text that determine the answer.

      b   Use the context to help identify the missing word.

6   Identify the ONE word that fits grammatically and in terms of sense.

7   If you are in any doubt about how to fill a gap, try sounding in your head how each potential word you have identified would fit.

8   On your Answer Sheet, clearly write ONE word in CAPITAL LETTERS for each gap. Check your spelling, as incorrect spelling is penalised.

9   Note the time when you have completed your answers.

How long did it take you to complete the questions?

Probably about 10 minutes? It is difficult to specify how long you should spend on any one Part, but in the Reading test as a rough guide you should aim to spend about 25-30 minutes on the first three Parts (36 marks), as the remaining three Parts require more reading time. This means you should spend no less than 8 minutes and no more than 10 minutes on a 12-mark Part such as this.

Don't worry if this Example took you longer than 10 minutes. Your speed will improve as you become familiar with the nature of the Parts and the approach you should take.

Study the correct answers to the Part 2 Example and make sure you understand the comments.

Answers to Part 2 Example

		Comments
0	THERE	This is the only *single* word that fits grammatically, following on from 'that'
13	FOR	These both test prepositions.
14	WITH	
15	WHO or THAT	A pronoun is needed here.
16	AT	A preposition is needed here.
17	WHICH	While many Part 2 tasks test at word or phrase level, this task requires you to understand the structure of the whole sentence.
18	SO	In this context 'so' quantifies how vaguely the objectives are drafted.
19	BE or GET	Either auxiliary verb is appropriate here.
20	THAN	The preceding word 'rather' determines 'than' here
21	ALL	A quantifier is needed here.
22	WHEN or IF	Both these questions test conjunctions and you should note that more than one answer is possible.
23	WHILE or WHILST or ALTHOUGH or THOUGH	
24	TO	A preposition is needed here.

Part 2 Full Practice Questions

Questions 13 - 24

▶ Read the following market report about the performance of investments.

▶ Identify the best word to fill each gap.

▶ For each question 13 – 24, write ONE word in CAPITAL LETTERS on your Answer Sheet.

There is an example at the beginning (0).

EXTRACT: MARKET REPORT

Period: for the six months ended 31 October

The period was profitable (0) ……….. investors in financial assets, with strong returns from the world's stock markets. For (13) ……….. most part, investors chose not to focus on the macroeconomic environment (14) ……….. rather on the impressive performance of companies as evidenced by strong profit growth around the world. Returns from fixed income assets were somewhat (15) ……… impressive but still strong (16) ……… historical terms. Europe was the region that provided returns towards the upper end of the spectrum, as ongoing successes in efforts to increase competitiveness by (17) ……… of cost cutting and restructuring activity impacted favourably on profits.

At the economic level, commentators spent much of the period focusing on whether or (18) ……… economic activity around the world remained on an upward trend, in particular in the USA. Overall, however, the consensus was that, in (19) ……… of some worrying indications in the first half of the year, expansion remained broadly (20) ……… track.

Looking ahead, (21) ……… is widely expected that the environment will be a challenging one for financial assets. The US economy, (22) ……….. looks set to slow during the coming year, will, as always, have an effect on the direction of the world economy. Most analysts agree that oil prices (23) ……… remain high – in the near term (24) ……… least – a fact that is likely to have an impact on corporate profitability.

Example answer:

0	F	O	R																	

Indicate your answers here in CAPITAL LETTERS:

13																	
14																	
15																	
16																	
17																	
18																	
19																	
20																	
21																	
22																	
23																	
24																	

(May 2007 paper)

Answers to Part 2 Full Practice Questions

		Comments
0	FOR	'Profitable for' is the grammatical phrase and fits the whole sentence.
13	THE	'For the most part' is a fixed phrase.
14	BUT	'But rather' fits grammatically in the context.
15	LESS	You may have thought that there was a range of possible answers for this question, including 'not', 'very' and 'more'. Note that neither 'not' nor 'very' can be preceded by 'somewhat'. 'More' does not fit in terms of the context: it is not possible for the returns to be 'more impressive but still strong in historical terms'.
16	IN	Knowledge of the fixed phrase 'in terms of' helps determine the missing word.
17	MEANS/WAY	When this was tested in May 2007 there was a wide range of wrong answers, including nouns such as 'method', 'introduction', 'expansion' and 'strategy'. These do not fit in the fixed phrase, which is 'by way of' or 'by means of'. The only way 'use' would fit would be to have 'the' in front of it ('by the use of '), and of course you are only allowed ONE word in this task.
18	NOT	'whether or not' is a fixed phrase
19	SPITE	If you thought the phrase should be 'in TERMS of' then you were not reading the full sentence to get the context. 'In spite of' is the only possible correct phrase for the context.
20	ON	'On track' is a fixed phrase.
21	IT	This is the only word that fits grammatically.
22	WHICH	If you wrote 'that' then you have recognized the need for a relative pronoun but have failed to recognise that in this particular clause the only possible answer was 'which'.
23	WILL	The context is clearly looking to the future tense here, so 'will' is appropriate.
24	AT	'At least' is a fixed phrase.

Part 3 introduction – forming a word

What do I have to do?

Read 2 short texts and complete 6 gaps in each one with ONE word each, formed by you from a given base word. Answers of more than one word will be marked wrong, even if they include the correct answer. Answers must be:

▶ grammatically correct at phrase and sentence level

▶ appropriate to the meaning of the whole text

▶ spelt correctly

How many questions/marks are there?

12 questions for 12 marks – 1 mark each (the Part is split into two 6-mark sections)

What texts are used?

Mainly extracts from reference books and financial textbooks, financial newspapers and journals, financial websites, company annual reports, research reports, correspondence and other documents.

What is being tested?

First that you understand the context of each gap in the text, so that you can decide which part of speech (noun, verb, adjective or adverb) is required, and, secondly, your ability to form that part of speech from the word given. The following may be required for instance:

▶ A plural form of a noun

▶ A specific part of a verb

▶ A negative prefix (eg 'un'-,' im'-, 'ir'-, 'dis'-, etc.)

▶ A compound eg produce 'countersign' from 'sign', or 'blacklist' from 'list'.

As a general rule, the word which conveys most meaning in the context is the word which is given to you as the base word.

How should I prepare for the Task?

▶ Read extensively

Part 3 introductory exercises (forming a word)

You should find these three introductory exercises helpful in relation to forming the appropriate parts of speech and understanding context.

Part 3 introductory exercise 1

You must be able to identify what part of speech – noun, adjective, verb or adverb – a gap in an extract requires, before you then go on to form the word.

In the following brief extract, <u>underline</u> the word that fits in each of the gaps.

'Professional accountants must follow the ***ethic/ ethical*** guidelines of the institute or association of which they are a member. Just behaving in a business-like ***manner/ mannerism/ manners*** is not sufficient. Most guidelines follow those laid down by IFAC, the ***globalization/ globular/ global*** organization of accountants. IFAC's core ***profess/ professional/ profession*** principles form the basis of a framework-based approach to ethics. Other systems which take a rule-based approach are ***argue/ arguably/ arguable*** more open to abuse by determined individuals seeking to find ways round the letter of the law. Accountants who have understood and learned to ***appreciative/ appreciation/ appreciate*** the function of the framework-based approach to ethics have generally found it to work well in practice.'

Part 3 introductory exercise 2

When forming words using prefixes you will find that these create negatives or opposites of the word given. When using suffixes you will often be creating a noun from a base word. In fact there are some very common prefixes and suffixes which perform these functions.

Using the prefixes in column A and the suffixes in column C, form the longest new word you can from each of the base words in column B. Write each one in column D. (Hints: you may have to make a minor spelling adjustment to the base word, and you will find there is one prefix and one suffix that cannot be used.)

A Prefixes	B Base word	C Suffixes	D New word(s)
In-	Success	-able	
Un-	Understand	-ful	
Im-	Legal	-ment	
Mis-	Agree	-ity	
Dis-	Possible	-ness	
Il-	Pay	-less	

Part 3 introductory exercise 3

Many nouns and verbs, or nouns and adjectives, are formed from the same identifiable stem.

Complete the table below by identifying the verb and/or the adjective that can be formed from the noun (we have completed the first one for you).

Noun	Verb	Adjective
nation	nationalise	national
advice		
globe		
profession		
value		
introduction		
choice		
difference		
competition		

Part 3 Answers to introductory exercises

Answers to Part 3 introductory exercise 1

'Professional accountants must follow the _ethical guidelines_ of the institute or association of which they are a member. Just behaving in a business-like _manner_ is not sufficient. Most guidelines follow those laid down by IFAC, the _global_ organization of accountants. IFAC's core _professional_ principles form the basis of a framework-based approach to ethics. Other systems which take a rule-based approach are _arguably_ more open to abuse by determined individuals seeking to find ways round the letter of the law. Accountants who have understood and learned to _appreciate_ the function of the framework-based approach to ethics have generally found it to work well in practice.'

Answers to Part 3 introductory exercise 2

A Prefixes	B Base word	C Suffixes	D New word(s)
In-	Success	-able	Un-success-ful
Un-	Understand	-ful	Mis-understand* Understand-able**
Im-	Legal	-ment	Il-legal-ity
Mis-	Agree	-ity	Dis-agree-ment
Dis-	Possible	-ness	Im-possib-ility***
Il-	Pay	-less	Pay-ment****

* To form a noun from 'misunderstand' you need to add '-ing', which was not available.

** You can't form a negative word from 'understandable'.

*** Note that with 'possible' the final two letters become 'il' when forming the noun with 'ity'

**** To form a negative noun from 'payment' you would have to have 'non-payment', but 'non-' was not available

Answers to Part 3 introductory exercise 3

Noun	Verb	Adjective
nation	nationalize	national
advice	advise	advisory
globe	globalize	global
profession	profess	professional
value	value	valuable
introduction	introduce	introductory
choice	choose	chosen
difference	differ/differentiate	different
competition	compete	competing

The style and format of the six Parts of the Reading test are very different. As it is quite a complicated test it's important that you become properly acquainted with each Part separately before tackling a Practice Test as a whole. We recommend therefore that you:

▶ Skim through the following Part 3 example, then the section on 'Getting started on the Part 3 Example' on page 46.

▶ Read through the section on 'How to approach the Part 3 example' on page 47 before completing the Part 3 Example and studying the answers on page 48, then

▶ Tackle the Part 3 Full Practice Questions on page 49.

Part 3 Example (forming a word)

▶ Read the following extract from a website article about the future of accountancy.

▶ Identify ONE new word to fill each numbered gap by using the word with the same number in the box below the text to form the new word.

▶ For each question 31 – 36, write ONE word in CAPITAL LETTERS on your Answer Sheet. Answers of more than one word will be marked wrong, even if they contain the correct answer.

EXTRACT: THE FUTURE FOR ACCOUNTANCY

The profession's future is certain to be more structured, ever more governed by global standards and under more scrutiny from a (31) .... of national and international bodies. Therefore accountants, particularly those working in small and medium practices, must change their mindset. They must start leading change; embrace (32) .... ; continuously improve their skills; invest in technology and demonstrate a fundamental (33) .... to professional ethics. Audit will be subjected to unprecedented scrutiny and auditors will have to expect to report on the (34) .... of their judgement and their lack of bias. Auditors will have to expect that they will be reporting on an organization's internal control (35) .... , but will also have to move rapidly to include detection of fraud as part of their audit report, otherwise markets will remain (36) .... about the value of audit.

31	VARY	32	INNOVATIVE
33	COMMIT	34	DEPENDENT
35	PROCEED	36	SCEPTIC

Indicate your answers here in CAPITAL LETTERS:

31																				
32																				
33																				
34																				
35																				
36																				

Getting started on the Part 3 Example

1   Where does the text come from?

It is an extract from a website article of unknown authorship and purpose.

2   What does the text deal with?

It deals with issues relating to the future of the accountancy profession, especially of audit.

How to approach the Part 3 Example

1   Note the time as you commence the Task.

2   Read the brief description of where the extract comes from at the beginning, and check that the requirement ('identify one new word to fill each numbered gap by using the word with the same number in the box below the text to form the new word') is what you expect.

3   Skim read the entire text very briefly for its gist.

4   Start to read the text more closely from the beginning. As you get to each gap, look closely at the words before and after it to recognize what is required (remember the gaps can be filled by referring just to the immediate phrase or sentence).

   a   Circle the word or words in the text that determine the answer.

   b   Use the context to help identify the missing part of speech (noun, verb, adjective or adverb)

   c   Look at the relevant given word and form from it ONE new word that is the appropriate part of speech, and that fits grammatically and in terms of sense.

5   If you are in any doubt about how to fill a gap, try sounding in your head how the potential word you have formed would fit.

6   On your Answer Sheet, clearly write ONE word in CAPITAL LETTERS for each gap. Check your spelling, as incorrect spelling is penalized.

7   Note the time when you have completed your answers.

How long did it take you to complete the questions?

Probably about 5 minutes? It is difficult to specify how long you should spend on any one Part, but in the Reading exam as a rough guide you should aim to spend about 25-30 minutes on the first three Parts (36 marks), as the remaining three Parts require more reading time. This means you should spend no less than 4 minutes and no more than 5 minutes on a 6-mark Part such as this.

Don't worry if this Example took you longer than 5 minutes. Your speed will improve as you become familiar with the nature of the Parts and the approach you should take.

Study the correct answers to the Part 3 Example and make sure you understand the comments.

Answers to Part 3 Example

		Comments
0	VARIETY	To form the noun 'variety' from the verb 'vary' you change the final 'y' to an 'i'. This is a common spelling rule that you should be aware of.
1	INNOVATION	Note that the 'e' at the end of the verb 'innovate' is dropped to form the noun 'innovation'. This is a common spelling rule that you should be aware of.
2	COMMITMENT	This is a simple suffixation of '-ment' to turn the verb 'commit' into the noun 'commitment'.
3	INDEPENDENCE	This task tests a prefix; the context requires 'independence' as opposed to 'dependence'. You need to read carefully and consider the possibility that, in addition to a change of part of speech, a prefix is required.
4	PROCEDURE(S)	The 'e' in 'proceed' is dropped to become 'procedures'. This is a common spelling rule that you should be aware of.
5	SCEPTICAL	This is a simple suffixation of '-al' to turn the noun 'sceptic' into the adjective 'sceptical'.

Note that:

▶ this Example only tests two different parts of speech (five nouns and one adjective); in the test adverbs and verbs may also be tested.

▶ this Example only tests affixation (adding letters at the beginning and/or end of words). Compounding may also be tested in Part 3, so that you form one word by adding two together.

Part 3 Full Practice Questions

Questions 25 – 30

▶ Read the following introduction to a book about international auditing standards.

▶ Use the words in the box below the text to form ONE word that fits in the same numbered gap in the text.

▶ For each question 25 – 30, clearly write ONE word in CAPITAL LETTERS on your Answer Sheet.

There is an example at the beginning (0).

EXAMPLE:

0	D	E	V	E	L	O	P	M	E	N	T									

EXTRACT: IMPLEMENTING INTERNATIONAL STANDARDS

A financial reporting system supported by strong governance, high-quality standards and sound regulatory frameworks is key to economic (0) ………. . Indeed, high quality standards of financial reporting, auditing and ethics underpin the trust that investors place in financial and non-financial information and, thus, play an integral role in a country's economic growth and financial (25) ……….

As the forces of (26) ………. prompt more and more countries to open their doors to foreign investment, and as business (27) ………. across borders becomes common, both the public and private sectors are (28) ………. recognizing the benefits of having a widely understood financial framework supported by strong, globally accepted auditing standards. The benefits of a global financial reporting framework are numerous and include: greater comparability of financial information for investors; greater (29) ………. on the part of investors to invest across borders; lower cost of capital; greater (30) ………. in the allocation of resources; and higher economic growth.

0	DEVELOP	25	STABLE	26	GLOBAL	27	EXPAND
28	INCREASE	29	WILLING	30	EFFICIENT		

Indicate your answers here in CAPITAL LETTERS:

25																			
26																			
27																			
28																			
29																			
30																			

(Sample paper)

Answers to Part 3 Full Practice Questions

		Comments
0	DEVELOPMENT	The context requires a noun and '-ment' is suffixed to 'develop' here.
25	STABILITY	Again a noun is needed; spelling rules dictate that 'stable' becomes 'stability'.
26	GLOBALISATION/ GLOBALIZATION	You may have puzzled over this, until you realised the context – especially 'foreign investment' and 'across borders' – demands 'globalization'.
27	EXPANSION	You could not grammatically use 'expands' here; the context requires a
28	INCREASINGLY	The context is 'are recognising' which suggests an adverb is needed.
29	WILLINGNESS	'Greater' is an adjective describing a noun, so 'willingness' fits.
30	EFFICIENCY	Again 'greater' requires a noun – 'efficiency'.

Part 4 introduction – skimming and scanning

What do I have to do?

Scan 6 paraphrased statements plus either a text which is divided into 4 sections, or 4 short texts, marked A, B, C and D, then match the statements with the relevant information from the text(s) by choosing one of the four options A, B, C or D. Some of the options will need to be used more than once.

How many questions/marks are there?

6 questions for 12 marks – 2 marks each.

What texts are used?

Mainly extracts from reference books and financial textbooks, financial newspapers and journals, financial websites, company annual reports, correspondence and other documents.

What is being tested?

Your general understanding of the gist of a text and the paraphrasing of key ideas, plus your ability to locate specific detailed information in the text. To do this you need to be able to skim for overall content and scan for specific information. To replicate a real-world situation where you know your purpose in reading a text, the statements to be matched appear before the texts.

How should I prepare for the task?

▶   Read extensively
▶   Refer to pages 7-10 for advice on reading ability, strategies and skills, and for advice on how to read faster.

Part 4 introductory exercise (skimming and scanning)

You should find this introductory exercise helpful in understanding how a piece of text is paraphrased in a brief statement.

Part 4 introductory exercise

Summarize each of the following unrelated texts in ONE sentence.

Text	Summary
Many businesses which made debt-funded acquisitions before the credit crunch need to reduce borrowing levels as soon as a possible as interest rates creep higher. Labour-intensive industries are concerned about wage bills as inflation starts to bite, while for all organizations oil prices and fuel consumption are very real concerns.	
Whilst every effort has been made to ensure that our review is as thorough as possible, we cannot be held responsible for errors and omissions in the accounts that have been deliberately concealed from us. It is the task of the company's management to ensure that transaction recording is done effectively and completely, and that controls are in place such that the information produced by the accounting system is reliable.	
A creditor of a company which has failed to pay its debt may decide to take legal action leading to the company declaring itself bankrupt. While this action in itself may prompt immediate payment of the outstanding debt there is a risk that instead it will trigger further legal and commercial consequences that in the end mean the debt remains unpaid. As far as possible therefore creditors are well-advised to negotiate settlements rather that initiate bankruptcy.	
Legally, anyone is free to advertise as an accountant and offer the full range of accountancy services. Members of a professional accountancy body are therefore open to competition from anyone, whether professionally qualified or not, who chooses to enter the market.	

Part 4 Answer to introductory exercise

Answer to Part 4 introductory exercise

Text	Summary
Many businesses which made debt-funded acquisitions before the credit crunch need to reduce borrowing levels as soon as possible as interest rates creep higher. Labour-intensive industries are concerned about wage bills as inflation starts to bite, while for all organisations oil prices and fuel consumption are very real concerns.	In today's economic climate businesses are struggling to contain costs.
Whilst every effort has been made to ensure that our review is as thorough as possible, we cannot be held responsible for errors and omissions in the accounts that have been deliberately concealed from us. It is the task of the company's management to ensure that transaction recording is done effectively and completely, and that controls are in place such that the information produced by the accounting system is reliable.	Directors have responsibility for the company's systems, controls and information.
A creditor of a company which has failed to pay its debt may decide to take legal action leading to the company declaring itself bankrupt. While this action in itself may prompt immediate payment of the outstanding debt, there is a risk that instead it will trigger further legal and commercial consequences that in the end mean the debt remains unpaid. As far as possible therefore creditors are well-advised to negotiate settlements rather that initiate bankruptcy.	Starting insolvency procedures is not the best way for creditors to get their money.
Legally, anyone is free to advertise as an accountant and offer the full range of accountancy services. Members of a professional accountancy body are therefore open to competition from anyone, whether professionally qualified or not, who chooses to enter the market.	The term 'accountant' enjoys no special position in law.

The style and format of the six Parts of the Reading test are very different. As it is quite a complicated test it's important that you become properly acquainted with each Part separately before tackling a Practice Test as a whole. We recommend therefore that you:

▶ Skim through the following Part 4 Example, then the section on 'Getting started on the Part 4 Example' on page 56.

▶ Read through the section on 'How to approach the Part 4 Example' on page 57 before completing the Part 4 Example and studying the answers on page 58, then

▶ Tackle the Part 4 Full Practice Questions on page 60.

Part 4 Example (skimming and scanning)

▶ Read the statements below and the extract from an article in a journal discussing the value of an MBA qualification for accountants on the opposite page.

▶ Identify which section of the extract (A, B, C or D) is referred to by each statement 37 – 42.

▶ For each question 37 – 42, mark ONE letter (A, B, C or D) on your Answer Sheet. You will need to use some of these letters more than once.

There is an example statement at the beginning (0).

Example:

0   The type of work that people in accountancy undertake is changing.

Answer:

0   **A** [ ]   **B** [-]   **C** [ ]   **D** [ ]

Statements:

37   Some people want to do an MBA because they do not already have a university degree.

38   An MBA can help people working in finance not to rely on purely numerical information.

39   People on an MBA course engage in practical as well as academic learning.

40   Possessing an MBA does not automatically lead to promotion.

41   An important part of doing an MBA is the contacts made on the course.

42   Where you take an MBA is of considerable importance.

EXTRACT: IS IT WORTH ACCOUNTANTS STUDYING FOR AN MBA?

A   As a business qualification the MBA (Master of Business Administration) degree has immense appeal to accountants. It is a highly respected qualification that can open many doors to the employment market, which were previously firmly shut. In general, business schools aim to provide MBA programmes that offer students from all backgrounds a thorough knowledge of the mechanics of management theory, encompassing human resources, finance, operations management, marketing and information systems. Lectures are coupled with regular group discussions, case studies and simulations.

B   Jane Baldwin, head of training with a large accountancy firm, is under no illusion that the marketplace for financial services is experiencing a period of transformation. 'No-one can stand still. As accountants, we've got to continue to develop our knowledge and skills. An MBA from any business school will equip graduates with a business element, a specialist element, and also help them to develop their interpersonal skills because the work that is done is not just as an individual but as a team as well,' says Baldwin. She also cites networking as a distinct advantage of an MBA programme.

C   As managing director of an international recruitment consultancy for finance professionals, Graham Simpson, however, has reservations about the importance of an MBA in the employment market. 'A lot of accountants ask us whether they should study for an MBA,' he begins. 'I would say that a number of them want to go for an MBA to compensate for some inadequacy they perceive themselves as having in the employment market.' The inadequacy he is referring to is the lack of a graduate qualification. Simpson admits that an MBA does have some value, but argues that the status of the business school is much more likely to get you a job than the MBA itself.

D   Someone who has recently completed an MBA is Michael Taylor, an international corporate tax specialist. Taylor chose to study for an MBA for the sake of his own personal development. Although he was recently made head of his department, he admits that, in his line of work, an MBA would not greatly enhance career progression. That said, he stresses that his studies enable him to empathise with his clients and offer a better service. 'I feel that taking an MBA prevents one from taking too narrow a view of one's professional duties. Having an MBA has allowed me to move away from just dealing with figures. If I use figures to back up what I say, then that's fine; but it doesn't matter if I don't as the qualitative issues may well be more important.'

Indicate your answers here:

37	A [ ]	B [ ]	C [ ]	D [ ]
38	A [ ]	B [ ]	C [ ]	D [ ]
39	A [ ]	B [ ]	C [ ]	D [ ]
40	A [ ]	B [ ]	C [ ]	D [ ]
41	A [ ]	B [ ]	C [ ]	D [ ]
42	A [ ]	B [ ]	C [ ]	D [ ]

Getting started on the Part 4 Example

You need to think about the following points once you've skimmed through the text and statements initially.

1 Where does the text come from?

It is taken from an article in a journal. It is continuous text that has been divided into four sections.

2 What does the text deal with?

The extract discusses the value of an MBA to members of the accountancy profession.

How to approach the Part 4 Example

1.   Note the time as you commence the task.

2.   Read the brief description of where the extract comes from at the beginning, and check that the requirement ('identify which section of the extract (A, B, C or D) is referred to by each statement') is what you expect.

3.   Read the example statement 0, the 6 statements 37-42 and all 4 texts together.

4.   Read Example Question 0 carefully and scan the 4 texts to check that you agree with the answer given (this will boost your confidence).

5.   Read each statement carefully and highlight key words in it, to help focus your reading and so that you know what specific information/key words to scan for in the texts. Next read the 4 texts to identify the one that the statement paraphrases. Don't select an answer solely on the basis of matching a word in the statement with a word in the text, as careful reading is required to ensure an accurate match in terms of meaning.

6.   On your Answer Sheet, for each of the 6 tasks make sure that you fill in just the lozenge related to your choice of option.

7.   Note the time when you have completed your answers.

How long did it take you to complete the questions?

Probably about 16 minutes? It is difficult to specify how long you should spend on any one Part, but in the Reading exam as a rough guide you should aim to spend about 45-50 minutes on the last three Parts (36 marks) as they require more reading time. Of the three, Part 4 probably demands the least time. This means you should spend no less than 15 minutes and no more than 16 minutes on the 12-mark Part 4.

Don't worry if this Example took you longer than 16 minutes. Your speed will improve as you become familiar with the nature of the Parts and the approach you should take.

Now study the correct answers to the Part 4 Example and make sure you understand the comments.

Answers to Part 4 Example

		Comments
0	**B**	You could have identified 'changing' as the key word in the statement, and matched it with 'transformation' and 'develop' in Text B. Occasionally, the same or similar words may be used in both the statement and the text but more commonly, as here, paraphrases are used.
37	**C**	You could have identified 'university degree' as the key words in the statement, and matched them with 'graduate qualification' in Text C.
38	**D**	Most of the quote from Michael Taylor in Text D is relevant to this statement. You need to understand the meaning of three sentences together here to match the statement to its text.
39	**A**	You should have identified 'academic' in the statement with 'lectures' in the text, and 'practical' in the statement with 'case studies' and 'simulations' in the text.
40	**D**	Note that the phrase 'does not automatically lead to promotion' in the statement paraphrases the phrase 'would not greatly enhance career progression' in Text D.
41	**B**	The word 'networking' in Text B is a more complex word than 'contacts' in the statement. Note that the wording of the statements in Part 4 is generally less complex than that of the texts.
42	**C**	The phrase 'status of the business school' in Text C is the key to the paraphrase 'where you take it' in the statement.

Part 4 Full Practice Questions

Questions 37 – 42

▶ Read the statement below and the extract about social responsibility accounting from a book about accounting and management on the opposite page.

▶ Which section (A, B, C or D) does each statement 37 – 42 refer to?

▶ For each question 37 – 42, mark ONE letter (A – D) on your Answer Sheet. You will need to use some of these letters more than once.

There is an example statement at the beginning (0).

Example:

0   The number of companies adopting social responsibility accounting has grown.

Answer:

0   **A** [-]   **B** [ ]   **C** [ ]   **D** [ ]

Statements:

37   Companies do not have to wait until they are forced to adopt socially responsible policies.

38   It is possible for social responsibility accounts to be presented in additon to standard financial reports.

39   The reputation of a company can be enhanced if it takes into account non-profit-making policies.

40   People are beginning to question previously held views about the main purpose of companies.

41   Some companies may produce reports that omit important details.

42   Socially responsible policies may prevent the closure of part of a company.

EXTRACT: SOCIAL RESPONSIBILITY ACCOUNTING

A   It is normally assumed that a company's overriding objective is profit maximization, however there are situations where profitability as the sole determinant of a company's policy is increasingly being challenged and even threatened. Public opinion and media reports are forcing companies to recognize that their shareholders are not the only stakeholders in the organization. Companies have a responsibility not only to make a profit for shareholders but also to take into account the needs and rights of other groups, such as employees, customers, local residents, environmental organizations and society as a whole. Many argue that, in the interests of social responsibility, companies should be willing to adjust some of their activities and incur greater costs. Measuring and reporting on these costs is becoming common practice, and is known as social responsibility accounting.

B   Acting responsibly and setting environmental and community objectives as well as financial ones has a positive side for a company as it can use its actions to gain valuable publicity as an organization which cares. A company will always be faced with the constraint of making enough profit to allow it to pay its shareholders enough dividend to encourage them to keep their shares and to buy new ones. However, it can also be required to behave in a way which takes other groups of people into account, and which recognizes other objectives besides financial ones.

C   In practice, companies try to balance conflicting interests against one another. Legislation requires companies to behave in certain socially and ethically acceptable ways, but it is also possible for them, on their own initiative, to go further than simply not breaking the law. For example, a company could decide to keep an unprofitable division because of a perceived commitment to the local community and perhaps a desire to avoid the resentment that results from job losses. Alternatively, a business could install pollution-reducing devices, thereby reducing profits, out of a sense of reponsibility to the environment and in response to local stakeholders, such as environmental pressure groups.

D   A profit-orientated organization can produce a social accounting statement alongside its normal financial statements. This can show the effects of its social policies and actions on the company's financial performance, the community and the environment. An attempt should be made to give a financial value to the social costs created, regardless of the difficulties involved. However, some companies confine themselves simply to giving a narrative of the social effects of their activities. Such narratives tend to state the positive actions being taken by the company without admiting to the negative ones. This might point to the advisability of an external audit being undertaken.

Indicate your answers here:

37	A [ ]	B [ ]	C [ ]	D [ ]
38	A [ ]	B [ ]	C [ ]	D [ ]
39	A [ ]	B [ ]	C [ ]	D [ ]
40	A [ ]	B [ ]	C [ ]	D [ ]
41	A [ ]	B [ ]	C [ ]	D [ ]
42	A [ ]	B [ ]	C [ ]	D [ ]

(May 2007 paper)

Answers to Part 4 Full Practice Questions

		Comments
0	**A**	This statement targets the first sentence of extract A.
37	**C**	The question targets the second sentence of section C, in particular the phrase 'on their own initiative'. You may have been tempted to match it with section A because of its fifth sentence (starting 'Many argue that…'). However, note that the emphasis of section A is companies' willingness to adopt socially responsible policies. This is not the same as companies being proactive in respect of social responsibility, which is the context of section C.
38	**D**	This paraphrases the first sentance of paragraph D.
39	**B**	You could match 'reputation… will be enhanced' with 'valuable publicity' in the first sentence of paragraph B.
40	**A**	'Main purpose' in the statement can be matched to 'sole determinant' in the first sentence of paragraph A.
41	**D**	The last half of paragraph D covers how companies 'omit important details' in order to look good.
42	**C**	This targets the third sentence of section C, in particular the phrase about keeping open 'an unprofitable division' which is a 'part of a company' as set out in the statement.

Part 5 introduction – understanding

What do I have to do?

Identify a sentence to fill each of 6 gaps in a single-page text (6 sentences have been removed from the text and placed in jumbled order after it, along with two other sentences). Choose one of the 8 options (A - H) to fill each of 6 gaps. In each case only one answer is correct.

How many questions/marks are there?

6 questions for 12 marks – 2 marks each.

What texts are used?

Texts with a strong development or argument are used for this task, and may be taken from reference books and financial textbooks, financial newspapers and journals, financial websites and research reports.

What is being tested?

You have to demonstrate an awareness of text structure, as well as understanding content, cohesion, coherence and global meaning. You must show your general understanding of a text and your ability to follow its detailed meaning and argument. To do this you must be able to recognise the function and meaning of contrast words used in arguments ('so', 'because', 'and', 'but' and 'or'). Part 5 is designed to test understanding of the development of ideas, opinions and events rather than the superficial recognition of individual words.

How should I prepare for the task?

▶ Read extensively
▶ Refer to pages 7-10 for advice on reading ability, strategies and skills, and for advice on how to read faster.

Part 5 introductory exercise (understanding)

You should find this introductory exercise helpful in appreciating how the logical argument of a text flows.

Part 5 introductory exercise

For each of the four sentences or phrases in column A below, select which of the two sentences or phrases in column B logically flows on from it. (Hint: you will find that the column B sentences/phrases offer a contrasting argument.)

A	B
Retailers now find themselves in the alarming situation of having excess inventory and customers who can no longer afford to shop.	1 As a result they are stocking up and expanding operations. 2 However, they are not in such a bad situation as housebuilders.
Acquisitions of plant and equipment during the period mean that the cost of fixed assets in the balance sheet has increased by 20%	1 but book values are only 10% higher given the change in depreciation policy. 2 because they were funded by a new issue of shares.
As a risk-averse investor you have, to date, avoided the stock market	1 so you have built up a substantial portfolio of shares. 2 but in fact it offers real opportunities for diversification
Setting a detailed budget for a period of longer than 12 months has limited value for most businesses	1 although it can be a helpful control mechanism if it is updated in light of events. 2 whereas cash flow is a vital performance indicator.

Part 5 Answer to introductory exercise

Answer to part 5 introductory exercise

A	B
Retailers now find themselves in the alarming situation of having excess inventory and customers who can no longer afford to shop.	2 However, they are not in such a bad situation as housebuilders.
Acquisitions of plant and equipment during the period mean that the cost of fixed assets in the balance sheet has increased by 20%	1 but book values are only 10% higher given the change in depreciation policy.
As a risk-averse investor you have, to date, avoided the stock market	2 but in fact it offers real opportunities for diversification
Setting a detailed budget for a period of longer than 12 months has limited value for most businesses	1 although it can be a helpful control mechanism if it is updated in light of events.

The style and format of the six Parts of the Reading test are very different. As it is quite a complicated test it's important that you become properly acquainted with each Part separately before tackling a Practice Test as a whole. We recommend therefore that you:

▶ Skim through the following Part 5 Example, then the section on 'Getting started on the Part 5 Example' on page 73.

▶ Read through the section on 'How to approach the Part 5 Example' on page 74 before completing the Part 5 Example and studying the answers on page 75, then

▶ Tackle the Part 5 Full Practice Questions on pages 76-77.

Part 5 Example (understanding)

▶ Read the following extract from an article on investigative due diligence and non-financial risk, and the sentences following the extract.

▶ Identify the best sentence to fill each of the gaps in the extract.

▶ For each gap 43 – 48, mark ONE letter (A – H) on your Answer Sheet. Do not use any letter more than once. There are two extra sentences which you do not need to use: sentence H is always used as the example at the beginning (0).

EXTRACT: INVESTIGATIVE DUE DILIGENCE AND NON-FINANCIAL RISK

Recent public disclosures of corporate fraud, unexpected company failure and business malpractice and corruption among well-known multinational companies highlight the need for transparency and solid understanding of the major risk from 'off balance sheet' issues. (0) .... This is especially true in areas where reliable, accurate business information is often unavailable and where a heavy reliance is placed on personal relationships and consequently on personal integrity. Managers are under considerable pressure to move to emerging markets and locations where core costs can apparently be reduced. But the evidence is that, in many such cases, key decisions are made based on incomplete or poor quality information, especially as regards people and politics.

When companies are considering a possible business partner, it is important that they know and understand the risks involved and how to eliminate, or at least minimise them. (43) .... Its specific goals are to unmask misrepresentation, reveal the undisclosed, clarify who you are dealing with and assess associated political and security risks.

Common problems that companies face include being overcharged for raw materials, billing discrepancies, unauthorised disposal of materials, fraudulent staff welfare claims and dummy employees, high transaction costs and other corrupt practices. (44) .... The key focus must be the people and entities involved in any potential transaction or joint venture: their background, reputation, track record and litigation history must be investigated. Today there are many new entrepreneurs who have excellent qualifications, skills and connections. (45)................

Investigative due diligence involves the collection, collation and analysis of information from a wide variety of sources. (46) .... This research should be supplemented by in-depth and discreet investigative field enquiries. The minimum that should be achieved through this is a thorough understanding of the actual corporate structure and the background and current activities of the professional management, key officers, shareholders and subsidiaries. Additionally, it will bring to light detailed information on the character, integrity and reputation of key individuals, as well as the company's reputation with associates in the same industry and its level of political support. (47) .... Other undisclosed issues, such as the use of 'sweatshop' labour or significant environmental issues that could lead to future losses or difficulties with licensing or permits, should also emerge.

Often these enquiries provide a completely different perspective from their conventional counterpart. Off balance sheet risk is manageable if companies are willing to adopt a robust approach to due diligence. Negative findings need not be a deal killer. (48) .... Due diligence is particularly cost-effective when undertaken early on in the deal-making process and not as an afterthought. It will identify issues to be addressed before committing to investing considerable financial expenditure and management resources.

Sentences:

A	To do this, they cannot just rely on introductions and meetings with middlemen, there has to be a process of investigative due diligence.
B	Such information can offer opportunities for more favourable terms to be negotiated and contracts structured to mitigate the risks identified.
C	As a result of this, it should be possible to identify any liabilities which do not appear on the balance sheet.
D	To avoid pitfalls such as these, it is critical that companies examine more than spreadsheets and legal documents.
E	It fails in its aim to identify business and political risks that are not visible or obvious.
F	However, this is not true of all of them and the lesson from many financial disasters is that it is vital to know the genuine people in business.
G	It starts with extensive multilingual data mining of publicly available material – specialist trade publications, online resources, media, public records, and corporate filings.
H	Such high profile cases mean that investors worldwide are discovering the danger of relying solely on audit reports and certified statements in making investment decisions.

Example answer:

0   A [ ]   B [ ]   C [ ]   D [ ]   E [ ]   F [ ]   G [ ]   H [-]

Indicate your answers here:

43	A [ ]	B [ ]	C [ ]	D [ ]	E [ ]	F [ ]	G [ ]	H [ ]
44	A [ ]	B [ ]	C [ ]	D [ ]	E [ ]	F [ ]	G [ ]	H [ ]
45	A [ ]	B [ ]	C [ ]	D [ ]	E [ ]	F [ ]	G [ ]	H [ ]
46	A [ ]	B [ ]	C [ ]	D [ ]	E [ ]	F [ ]	G [ ]	H [ ]
47	A [ ]	B [ ]	C [ ]	D [ ]	E [ ]	F [ ]	G [ ]	H [ ]
48	A [ ]	B [ ]	C [ ]	D [ ]	E [ ]	F [ ]	G [ ]	H [ ]

Getting started on the Part 5 Example

You need to think about the following points once you've skimmed through the text and sentences initially.

1   Where does the text come from?

It is taken from an article in a journal. It is a continuous text from which a total of 7 complete sentences have been removed (one of them is used as an example).

2   What is the text about?

It is about investigative due diligence and its role in the assessment of non-financial risk.

How to approach the Part 5 Example

How to approach the task

1   Note the time as you commence the task.

2   Read the brief description of where the extract comes from at the beginning, and check that the requirement ('identify the best sentence to fill each of the gaps in the extract') is what you expect.

3   Carefully read the entire extract to get an idea of the structure, meaning and development of its theme before starting to do the tasks. You should read it without looking at the sentences so you become familiar with its content and development, and so that you know what to look out for in the sentences.

4   Read the first paragraph of the extract, and check that you agree that Sentence H is the correct answer (this will boost your confidence).

5   For each numbered gap in the rest of the extract, read the paragraph around it carefully at least twice, noting in particular the information and ideas that appear before and after each gap.

    a   The option you select to fill the gap must fit the text before the gap, and equally importantly must allow the text after the gap to follow on coherently.

    b   Don't simply match a sentence with a part of the text that contains the same word or phrase. It is your understanding of the development of ideas, opinions and events that is being tested, not your superficial ability to recognise individual words.

    c   Tick off each sentence as you fit it into the extract. Once you have done the task, you should always check that the extra sentence doesn't fit anywhere.

6   On your Answer Sheet, for each of the 6 tasks make sure that you fill in just the lozenge related to your choice of option: A, B, C or D.

7   Note the time when you have completed your answers.

How long did it take you to complete the questions?

Probably about 18 minutes? It is difficult to specify how long you should spend on any one Part, but in the Reading test as a rough guide you should aim to spend about 45-50 minutes on the last three Parts (36 marks) as they require more reading time. Of the three, Part 5 probably demands the most time. This means you should spend no less than 16 minutes and no more than 18 minutes on the 12-mark Part 5.

Don't worry if this Example took you longer than 18 minutes. Your speed will improve as you become familiar with the nature of the Parts and the approach you should take.

Now study the correct answers for the Part 5 Example and make sure you understand the comments.

Answers to Part 5 Example

		Comments
0	**H**	Remember that sentence H is always the one that fills the example gap 0 in this Part.
43	**A**	Notice the preceding sentence says: 'When companies are considering a possible business partner...'. To find the right completing sentence, look for one which relates to ways of going about this. Sentence A says: 'To do this … there has to be a process of investigative due diligence'. You need to check the text after the gap as well however; this begins, 'Its specific goals are…'. 'Its' needs to refer back to a singular noun in the gap, namely 'process' in Sentence A. You should always check that the sentence you choose fits grammatically. It is possible to eliminate some of the sentences A – G on this basis; for example, in Sentence D there is no singular noun.
44	**D**	The preceding sentence lists common problems, so sentence D – beginning 'to avoid pitfalls such as these' – fits well here.
45	**F**	'However' in Sentence F is an example of a linking device signalling contrast, commonly tested in Part 5. Similar phrases to do with contrast are: 'on the other hand', 'conversely', 'although', 'whereas', and 'but'. Note that 'them' in Sentence F matches the plural 'entrepreneurs' in the sentence preceding the gap.
46	**G**	To fill this gap you are looking for some 'research' that the subsequent sentence points out 'should be supplemented'. Sentence G refers to 'extensive multilingual data mining' and therefore fits very well.
47	**C**	'As a result of' is a linking phrase signalling the effect of something such as a course of action. Cause and effect are key areas in Part 5.
48	**B**	'Such information' in sentence B refers back to 'negative findings' in the previous sentence.

Part 5 Full Practice Questions

Questions 43 – 48

▶ Read the following website article about the analytical skills needed by accountants.

▶ Choose the best sentence to fill each of the gaps.

▶ For each gap 43 – 48, mark one letter (A – H) on your Answer Sheet. Do not use any letter more than once. There is one extra sentence which you do not need to use.

There is an example statement at the beginning (0).

EXTRACT: ANALYTICAL FINANCIAL SKILLS FOR TOMORROW'S ACCOUNTANTS

As a finance professional you need to support your employers or clients with a range of analytical skills. (0) .... Depending on your role, you may have to check the accounts of a UK retail outlet with a £250,000 turnover, looking for indications of payroll fraud, or undertake due diligence in a Malaysian mergers and acquisitions bid, to analyse potential problem areas in terms of information systems integration. If you work in industry, you may be required to analyse budget variances for the product lines in the tube manufacturing unit of an Indian steel producer. (43) .... You cannot possibly be all things to everyone so, unless you are determined to specialize in a particular area, you need to develop the analytical skills that will be most portable.

Fortunately, many of the skills developed while working on one type of analysis will be useful while working on others; in particular, general purpose spreadsheet skills remain in huge demand. But, according to Susan Hoof, an accountancy teacher, many students will be capable of producing a spreadsheet, but be unable to work with the data and use formulae. (44) .... For example, a junior financial modeller in the analysis team of a financial services organization will need to be more familiar with the details of spreadsheet software, such as Excel, than a group financial accountant will – and the further up the career ladder you climb, the less likely you are to need this skill. (45) .... Analysis is more about interpretation and perspective than number crunching, and potential employers look for soft skills as well as technical expertise. If interpretation skills, or the ability to demonstrate them, are lacking, then all the technical and software knowledge in the world will be insufficient to make you a good analyst.

On a technical level general ledger work, transaction processing and financial analysis all require different financial skills sets and approaches, plus a selection of soft skills. (46) .... But recently qualified accountants often lack these skills and have problems with report writing. They do not understand what information is expected, or the way in which it should be presented. (47) ....

The level of complexity of information that a finance professional can assimilate will be very different from that which the marketing director or human resource manager can deal with. (48) .... Similarly, the way financial information is conveyed to those inside and outside a company should differ, not just in terms of what is acceptable or appropriate, but because varying levels of background knowledge or industry expertise must be accommodated.

---

0   **A** [ ]   **B** [ ]   **C** [ ]   **D** [ ]   **E** [ ]   **F** [ ]   **G** [ ]   **H** [-]

Sentences:

A	It is important therefore that all members of the financial analysis group, when addressing non-finance stakeholders within the company, avoid the tendency to present numbers without providing insight into what they mean.
B	This lack of expertise need not be a problem, however, as what is expected by an employer will range widely, depending on factors such as role and salary.
C	The latter are especially important for those in the financial analysis group where accountants need to be able to communicate effectively with non-finance staff.
D	These different situations will call for different types of financial analysis and a selection of complementary, non-financial skills.
E	Until then, accountants should not even start to look at the numbers and produce the required analysis.
F	Many fail to present implications clearly and concisely, and in the format that best suits the audience at which a document is aimed.
G	Even so, those who want to progress should spend some time ensuring they are comfortable using such tools and capable of taking the data they contain and turning it into business information.
H	But the ones that will prove most useful will depend on the direction you choose to take in your career.

Indicate your answers here:

43	**A** [ ]	**B** [ ]	**C** [ ]	**D** [ ]	**E** [ ]	**F** [ ]	**G** [ ]	**H** [ ]
44	**A** [ ]	**B** [ ]	**C** [ ]	**D** [ ]	**E** [ ]	**F** [ ]	**G** [ ]	**H** [ ]
45	**A** [ ]	**B** [ ]	**C** [ ]	**D** [ ]	**E** [ ]	**F** [ ]	**G** [ ]	**H** [ ]
46	**A** [ ]	**B** [ ]	**C** [ ]	**D** [ ]	**E** [ ]	**F** [ ]	**G** [ ]	**H** [ ]
47	**A** [ ]	**B** [ ]	**C** [ ]	**D** [ ]	**E** [ ]	**F** [ ]	**G** [ ]	**H** [ ]
48	**A** [ ]	**B** [ ]	**C** [ ]	**D** [ ]	**E** [ ]	**F** [ ]	**G** [ ]	**H** [ ]

(May 2007 Paper)

Answers to Part 5 Full Practice Questions

		Comments
0	**H**	Remember that sentence H is always the one that fills the example gap in this Part.
43	**D**	'These different situations' in D clearly refers back to the different roles outlined in the previous two sentences.
44	**B**	This sentence has strong backwards and forwards links. 'This lack of expertise' in B refers backwards to 'unable to work with' in the preceding sentence, while 'what is expected by an employer' in B refers forwards to the example in the subsequent sentence of different roles and the necessary skills. You may have been tempted to select sentence F, which fits the preceding sentence but is ruled out by the following one.
45	**G**	'Such tools' refers back to 'spreadsheet software'.
46	**C**	Note that 'the latter' at the beginning of sentence C refers back to 'soft skills' in the preceding sentence. If you were tempted by the context to select sentence G, you should have noticed that 'Even so' at its start rules this out. In addition, one could not refer to 'general ledger work, transactions processing and financial analysis' as 'tools'.
47	**F**	'Many' refers back to 'qualified accountant' in the preceding sentence.
48	**A**	You need to understand the context fully to identify the correct answer here. The preceding sentence implies that marketing and HR managers can only cope with less complex information – which feeds into finance professionals needing to present numbers with insight into what they mean.

Part 6 introduction – interpreting

What do i have to do?

Read one single-page text and answer 6 multiple-choice questions about it. The questions are presented in the same order as the information in the text. You should read each question very carefully, as well as its 4 possible answers.

How many questions/marks are there?

6 questions for 12 marks – 2 marks each.

What texts are used?

Texts usually contain some opinion or analysis of practices/events and are mainly taken from reference books and financial textbooks, financial newspapers and journals, financial websites, and research reports.

What is being tested?

You have to display detailed understanding of a text and the opinions expressed in it, and you must be able to interpret opinion and inference. You need to read the text closely for detail, opinion, implication and referencing in order to distinguish between, for example, apparently similar viewpoints, outcomes or reasons. There may also be a question focusing on the meaning of a particular word or phrase in the text, or on a reference word such as a pronoun.

How should I prepare for the task?

▶   Read extensively

▶   Refer to pages 7-10 for advice on reading ability, strategies and skills, and for advice on how to read faster.

▶   Skim through the following Part 6 Example, then the section on 'Getting started on the Part 6 Example' on page 84.

▶   Read through the section on 'How to approach the Part 6 Example' on page 85 before completing the Part 6 Example and studying the answers on page 87, then

▶   Tackle the Part 6 Full Practice Questions on page 88.

Part 6 Example (interpreting)

▶ Read the following extract from a text about budgeting, and the questions following the extract.

▶ Identify the best option as the answer to each question on the basis of what you have read in the extract.

▶ For each question 49 – 54, mark ONE letter (A, B, C or D) on your Answer Sheet for the answer you choose.

EXTRACT: COMPANY BUDGETS

Most senior executives know that the competitive battles ahead will involve not only ensuring that their company gets better at what it does, but is also different from others. To achieve this they need talented managers who can produce more imaginative strategies for growth and improvement, make faster decisions, be more flexible, be better prepared to anticipate threats and opportunities, and who can consistently improve quality and customer satisfaction. To this list you can add any number of other key competitive issues that are becoming more important as the service economy gathers speed.

But executives also know that none of these aspirations are attainable without changing the way the business is run. While most companies have tried to address these issues by reducing management layers and focusing on the customer, few have been successful. One of the reasons is the inability to shift the management philosophy from one of top-down control to bottom-up empowerment. It is because budgets are most commonly used by organizations to exercise control that they are at the centre of this thorny issue.

Budgets are, in effect, barriers to change and fail to do well what most managers think they do well – that is, provide order and control. They are barriers for many reasons. Firstly, they reinforce the command and control management model and thus undermine attempts at organizational change, such as delegation and empowerment. In addition, they tend to set a ceiling on growth potential and a floor for cost reductions, thus stifling real improvement breakthroughs. Strong brands, skilled people, excellent management processes, strong leadership, and loyal customers are assets that are outside the measurement orbit of the accounting system. Budgets are typically extrapolations of existing trends, with little attention being paid to anticipatory models. What is more, they act as barriers to exploiting cooperation across the business units.

If asked why we use budgets, most managers would probably answer, 'to set targets and control business operations'. But budgets evolved in the 1920s to help growing businesses manage their capital resources and plan their cash requirements. It was not until the 1960s that budgets were used to set targets, control operations and evaluate managerial performance. While planning remains an important part of the management process, it is widely believed that setting targets and controlling and evaluating performance using budgets is fundamentally flawed because it directs managerial behaviour towards achieving predetermined financial targets rather than harnessing the energy of people at all levels towards continuously improving competitive strategies and customer-oriented processes.

So, if existing budgeting systems have such crucial weaknesses, why do we still rely on them? In fact, accountants have tried to improve them. Zero-based budgeting and activity-based budgeting represent valiant efforts to update the process, but they tend to be complex project-driven approaches that fail to evolve into standard management practices. Basically, though, budgeting has not changed because it is a part of unchallenged tradition. Some companies are re-engineering their budgeting processes to make them faster and cheaper, but such an approach fails the test, as it leaves the behavioural weaknesses in place.

What does all this mean for the role of management accountants? Many accountants now accept that setting fixed financial targets and measuring performance against them makes little sense when the competitive environment is subject to continuous change. Plans and strategies need to unfold continuously as new knowledge emerges. Above all, management accountancy should be concerned with the future and ensuring that the right questions are asked and the right decisions are taken that add maximum long-term value. It is hard, though, to see how these changes can be managed successfully while leaving the current budgeting system in place.

Questions:

49   To deal with the competition they are likely to meet in the future, companies should look for managers who will

      A   recognize and reward talented people.

      B   bring considerable experience to the job.

      C   respond immediately to financial difficulties.

      D   take a creative approach to developing the business.

50   According to the second paragraph, why have companies failed in their response to key competitive issues?

A   Authority for decision-making is too restricted.

B   Customer needs are not given sufficient priority.

C   There are too many layers of management.

D   Budgets are not adequately monitored.

51   One problem resulting from the way budgets are usually set is that:

A   they give too optimistic a view of a company's growth potential.

B   they allow staff to avoid taking responsibility for their decisions.

C   they tend to produce too many targets for the workforce to meet.

D   they limit innovative behaviour because they focus on past experience.

52   According to the writer, changes in the use of budgets since the 1960s have prevented managers from

A   giving enough time to planning.

B   concentrating on motivating the workforce.

C   working out realistic targets.

D   assessing the competence of their employees.

53   According to the writer, why have new budgeting systems not been widely adopted?

A   Traditional systems are relatively easy to operate.

B   New systems have proved slow and expensive.

C   Traditional systems are part of accepted practice.

D   New systems have proved unpopular with managers.

54   According to the final paragraph, many management accountants now believe that

    A   companies should be prepared to modify their strategies.

    B   budgeting should not influence management decisions.

    C   too many company decisions are taken with a short-term view.

    D   targets should reflect recent trends in an industry sector.

Indicate your answers here:

49	A [ ]	B [ ]	C [ ]	D [ ]
50	A [ ]	B [ ]	C [ ]	D [ ]
51	A [ ]	B [ ]	C [ ]	D [ ]
52	A [ ]	B [ ]	C [ ]	D [ ]
53	A [ ]	B [ ]	C [ ]	D [ ]
54	A [ ]	B [ ]	C [ ]	D [ ]

(Sample paper)

Getting started on the Part 6 Example

You need to think about the following point once you've skimmed through the text (NOT the questions) initially.

1   Where does the text come from?

It is taken from a text on budgeting.

2   What is the text about?

It is about the role of company budgets in a competitive environment

How to approach the Part 6 Example

How to approach the task

1   Note the time as you commence the Task.

2   Read the brief description of where the extract comes from at the beginning, and check that the requirement ('identify the best option as the answer to each question') is what you expect.

3   Carefully read the entire extract to get an idea of the structure, meaning and development of its theme. You should read it WITHOUT LOOKING AT THE QUESTIONS so you become familiar with its content and development. As three of the four options in each question are incorrect, there is little point in trying to absorb them all before tackling the text.

4   Taking each question in turn:

    a   Read the question very carefully WITHOUT looking at the options, that is answer it as an open question. You may find that your answer matches one of the options, in which case there is a strong possibility that this is the right answer.

    b   Read each option very carefully and check each in turn against the evidence of the text.

        i   In the case of items which take the form of an incomplete sentence, the completed sentence created by matching it to an option must match what is written in the text, and not just the option itself.

        ii   Don't simply match words in the text with words in the question or option. Careful study of the questions and text is very important.

5   On your Answer Sheet, for each of the 6 tasks make sure that you fill in just the lozenge related to your choice of option, A, B, C or D.

6   Note the time when you have completed your answers.

How long did it take you to complete the questions?

Probably about 18 minutes? It is difficult to specify how long you should spend on any one Part, but in the Reading test as a rough guide you should aim to spend about 45-50 minutes on the last three Parts (36 marks) as they require more reading time. Part 6 probably demands as much time as Part 5 as the extract is so long. This means you should spend no less than 16 minutes and no more than 18 minutes on the 12-mark Part 6. The text for this Part is particularly dense, and consequently hard to process. The questions require a lot of thought and, often, words from the text are used to 'distract' you, so you must leave yourself adequate time to complete this task.

Don't worry if this Example took you longer than 18 minutes. Your speed will improve as you become familiar with the nature of the Parts and the approach you should take.

Now study the correct answers for the Part 6 Example and make sure you understand the comments.

Answers to Part 6 Example

		Comments
49	**D**	Remember that the questions follow the order of the text so you are justified in searching the first paragraph for the answer to this question. You can only select the correct option if you are prepared to summarise the second sentence in your own mind on being about 'creativity' in developing the business.
50	**A**	The question refers to most of the second paragraph, to which you are referred. Although the answer is mainly rooted in the third sentence, it is necessary to process the text from 'none of these aspirations are attainable' in the first sentence to 'budgets are most commonly used ....to exercise control' in order to be certain of the correct answer.
51	**D**	The answer is not located solely in the penultimate sentence of the third paragraph. Although you can deduce from the penultimate sentence that budgets focus on past experience, you need to look earlier in the third paragraph (to 'attempts at organisational change' and 'stifling real improvement breakthroughs') to understand that budgets limit innovative behaviour.
52	**B**	This question targets the fourth paragraph. The correct answer can be identified by a process of elimination. 'Planning', 'targets' and 'assessing', according to the writer, are negative aspects of the budgetary process – so motivation must be what has been prevented.
53	**C**	The incomplete sentence in the question and answer paraphrase the fifth paragraph. The text says 'Zero-based budgeting and activity-based budgeting represent valiant efforts to update the process .....Basically, though, budgeting has not changed because it is a part of unchallenged tradition'. The question asks 'Why have new budgeting systems not been widely adopted?', so the correct option is 'Traditional systems are part of accepted practice'.
54	**A**	This question tests the opinion of accountants as reported in the text.

Part 6 Full Practice Questions

Questions 49 – 54

▶ Read the following extract from a research document about disclosure in company reports, and the following questions.

▶ Identify the best option as the answer to each question on the basis of what you have read in the extract

▶ For each question 49 – 54, mark ONE letter (A, B, C or D) on your Answer Sheet for the answer you choose.

EXTRACT: DISCLOSURE IN COMPANY REPORTS

This report presents the results of a research project concerned with discretionary financial disclosures by UK companies. The main purpose of the research was to examine the extent to which the publication of forward-looking information in the annual reports of companies is associated with the interest shown in these reports by professional financial analysts. This research forms part of a broader project that is concerned with the causes and consequences of voluntary financial disclosures, and the quality of financial communication between companies and investment professionals.

In stock market-based economies, such as the US and the UK, the informed pricing of corporate securities is vital for economic stability and the promotion of sustained levels of high quality investment by corporations. During the 1990s, doubt was cast on the usefulness of conventional measures of financial performance as a basis for fundamental valuation. Prior to this, financial indicators of performance such as earnings and book value per share had generally been perceived as providing a useful starting point for company valuation.

The diminishing relevance of conventional accounting indicators has manifested itself in two related ways. First, we have witnessed an increased tendency for many firms to publish more forward-looking information in their annual report. Indeed, reports do seem to have increased materially in length in recent years, mostly in the unaudited, qualitative, and forward-looking sections of the report. Companies, it would appear, have recognised the limitations of the conventional indicators, and have produced alternative forms of information to address them. A number of researchers have also discovered that the ability of accounting earnings and book values to explain company valuations, or changes in valuation over time, has declined.

For this research, we constructed an index of forward-looking financial disclosures based on a detailed analysis of the annual reports of 57 UK companies. Our analysis revealed considerable differences in company practice. By using a scoring system, we found that the amount of material disclosed ranged between 17 items for the least forthcoming company and 111 for the most forthcoming one. A practical problem was that the technique was costly to implement. We estimated that each annual report took about 0.5 days to score. In our second study we took a sample of 230 companies for two financial years in a row. To avoid the costs of scoring 460 annual reports, we used the page length of the annual report as a crude proxy for disclosure quality. Since most firms' annual reports adopt a similar format from one year to another, the page length gives a fairly sensitive indication of firms that have changed their disclosure stance.

Using standard econometric modelling methods, we tested whether increases in page length were either preceded by or followed by associated changes in analyst forecasting activity. Our findings revealed the richness of the communications that now routinely take place within the unregulated portions of the annual report. The results indicated a statistically significant increase in analyst forecasting activity. Ordinary investors find it helpful to know about the range of indicators that drive professional investment opinion. Some finance directors, though, may be interested to learn that increased analyst attention appears to carry a 'price', in terms of the need to increase the quality of forward-looking information available to this class of user.

The research produced evidence consistent with our view that one of the main considerations driving the financial disclosure choices of UK companies is the need to supply forward-looking, value-relevant information to professional financial analysts. There was a statistically significant increase in page length following an increase in analyst forecasting activity, although there was some evidence of the reverse effect, as a slight tendency was noted for analyst forecasting activity to rise following an increase in the page length of the annual report. These results, though, do run counter to the evidence reported for the New York stock market.

Questions:

49   The research project was set up to investigate whether financial disclosure by a company is

    A   likely to provide financial analysts with data they will find useful.

    B   linked to the attention that financial analysts pay to this information.

    C   responsible for the recommendations made by financial analysts.

    D   relevant to forward-planning decisions made by financial analysts.

50   According to the second paragraph, what happened with regard to company valuation in the 1990s?

    A   New methods of establishing this were introduced.

    B   Uncertainty was expressed about its importance.

    C   It became almost impossible to arrive at an accurate estimate.

    D   The traditional ways of assessment were called into question.

51   What does the third paragraph tell us about companies' annual reports?

    A   There is no longer a requirement for certain parts of the report to be audited.

    B   The manner in which they deal with past performance has changed.

    C   There is an increase in the amount of space devoted to future expectations.

    D   They are required to include material concerned with forward-looking information.

52   In their studies, the researchers used page length to assess the amount of forward-looking disclosures because

    A   there is very little variation in page length from one year to the next.

    B   the earlier method of assessment had resulted in a large number of variations.

    C   assessing page length gives a clear indication of the reliability of the information.

    D   the method of assessment they used originally was too time-consuming.

53   According to the fifth paragraph, the forward-looking material that now appears in many company reports

    A   can provide shareholders with useful information.

    B   needs to be limited so as to prevent costs from rising.

    C   has benefited from being more strictly controlled.

    D   should principally address the interests of financial analysts.

54   What does the final paragraph say about the results of the research?

    A   They were broadly in line with results from research in the US.

    B   They were regarded as being inconclusive.

    C   They came as no surprise to the researchers.

    D   They confirmed that analysts' predictions are reliable.

Indicate your answers here:

49	**A** [ ]	**B** [ ]	**C** [ ]	**D** [ ]
50	**A** [ ]	**B** [ ]	**C** [ ]	**D** [ ]
51	**A** [ ]	**B** [ ]	**C** [ ]	**D** [ ]
52	**A** [ ]	**B** [ ]	**C** [ ]	**D** [ ]
53	**A** [ ]	**B** [ ]	**C** [ ]	**D** [ ]
54	**A** [ ]	**B** [ ]	**C** [ ]	**D** [ ]

(May 2007 paper)

Answers to Part 6 Full Practice Questions

		Comments
49	**B**	The question and options target the second sentence of the first paragraph, where the main purpose of the research is explained. If you were tempted to select option D you may have been focusing on 'forward-looking planning decisions' in the option and tying that up with 'forward-looking information' in the first part of the sentence. In fact the answer is to be found in its second part.
50	**D**	'Calling into question' traditional methods is echoed in the phrase 'doubt was cast on the usefulness of conventional measures'.
51	**C**	'An increase in the amount of space .... future expectations' echoes 'publish more forward-looking information' in the third paragraph. If you were tempted to answer D you should note that there is nothing in the paragraph suggesting legislation, regulation or compulsion, so companies cannot have been 'required' to include more material.
52	**D**	The fourth paragraph covers research methods and the amount of time spent – and option D is the only one to mention this.
53	**A**	'Shareholders' in option A relates to 'ordinary investors' in the paragraph.
54	**C**	The question and options target the beginning of the last paragraph. If you were tempted to answer A to this you may have failed to realize that the last sentence of the paragraph means that in fact the results were *not* in line with results from US research.

Writing

Contents of the Writing section

Introduction to Writing

Overview of the Writing Test

Test format

The paper consists of two compulsory finance-related tasks: a letter and a report written in response to information provided and for a given purpose and target reader. The finance-related tasks are ones that practitioners would expect to meet in their daily working lives.

Timing

1 hour and 15 minutes in total.

Marks

Part 1 (a letter) carries 40% and Part 2 (a report) carries 60% of the marks available.

Answers

You must write your answers on the question paper, in which you will be given lined pages at the appropriate points. Your emphasis should be on effective communication with the target reader.

Summary of the Writing Test

Part	Task Type and Focus	Number of Tasks/Length	Format and Focus
1	Write a letter in response to letter received (an input letter) plus five notes.	1 compulsory task 120 -180 words in total*	In the letter you must use a range of vocabulary and structure, as defined by the task.
2	Write a report based on a context plus four content points, developing finance-related topics and discussing finance-related issues in a non-technical way.	1 compulsory task 200 – 250 words in total*	In the report you have more scope to display your language and communication skills as there is more flexibility in content.

Important notes:

*Expected word length

You are asked to write 120–180 words for Part 1 and 200–250 words for Part 2 (and the test booklet doesn't leave you space to write much more). Try very hard to stick to the expected word length as over-length or under-length answers will be penalised:

▶   using significantly fewer words is likely to mean that the task has not been completed,

▶   over-long pieces of writing may involve irrelevance or have a negative effect on the target reader. They also take longer to check and therefore tend to contain more uncorrected errors.

Irrelevance

The examiners want to give credit for your efforts at communication, but you'll be penalised for content that is irrelevant to the task set, because in the real world this would have a negative impact on the target reader and would interfere with successful communication.

Do's & Don'ts in the Writing Test

	When planning your answer
	DO

✓	Read **each question** very carefully.
✓	**Underline** or **highlight** the most important points in the rubric and input for each task.
✓	Decide exactly what **information** you are being asked to give.
✓	Identify the **person** you are writing to and the overall **purpose** of what you have to write.
✓	**Organise** your ideas and make a **plan** before you write.
✓	For the letter task, think carefully about how to **link the five notes**.
✓	For the report task, think carefully about the **balance of the four content points** – which can be expanded and which can be dealt with more concisely?

	DON'T
✗	Don't start writing before you have finished your planning.
✗	Don't 'lift' too much language from the input.

When writing	
DO	
✓	Write your answers in the question booklet provided.
✓	Write legibly.
✓	Write in a formal / neutral style.
✓	Concentrate on communicating effectively via your writing.
✓	Organise your ideas into clear paragraphs.
✓	Follow your plan and remember the overall purpose of what you are writing.
✓	Use as wide a range of complex structures and vocabulary as you can.
✓	Use a variety of linking words and ensure that the flow of ideas is logical and easy for the reader to follow.
✓	Allow time for checking and revising what you have written, neatly.

DON'T	
✗	Don't just list information in simple sentences
✗	Don't use an inappropriate style or tone - it is not specifically penalised but may mean that the overall mark is adjusted as the wrong impression has been given.
✗	Don't worry if you make mistakes, just ensure they are neatly and clearly corrected.
✗	Don't worry excessively about spelling errors as they are not penalized unless they are 'impeding' errors, that is if they impede communication.
✗	Don't worry about whether you use American or British usage and spelling, but be consistent.
✗	Don't write much more than the expected word length in each part – you shouldn't include irrelevant material.

When you have finished writing	
DO	
✓	Check that you have covered all the notes and content points.
✓	Check for spelling and punctuation errors. Even if errors don't impede communication they may affect the overall impact of the message.
✓	Make sure that you have crossed out any errors and that the final version is easy to read.
✓	Make clear corrections so the examiner can follow and mark what you have written.

Preparation for the Writing Test

Think about the balance between the target reader and the letter/report's function

Each letter and each report will have a target reader and a specific function. You need to write to/for them in an appropriate style and tone. You'll find guidance on this later in this Workbook.

Practise writing in financial English

The best preparation for the Writing paper is to practise writing letters and reports on finance-related topics in English so as to communicate effectively with the target reader.

You should therefore aim to practise:

▶ Identifying the overall function of a task (the 'bigger picture').

▶ Reformulating language from note form to full sentences.

▶ Reformulating language from informal to formal expressions.

▶ Making a brief plan for a letter or a report which:

  – addresses the correct points

  – is well-balanced so you can demonstrate a range of language

  – demonstrates a logical flow of ideas.

▶ Writing letters and reports in your own handwriting within the word limit so you'll be aware of when you have written up to the limit.

▶ Writing letters and reports that 'hold together' properly, in particular:

  – using a separate paragraph to develop each identifiable point

  – writing freely using linking words effectively

  – developing a logical argument

  – having a proper introduction and conclusion reflecting the bigger picture

▶ Developing points as fully as possible when writing to demonstrate a range of language.

▶ Using a variety of vocabulary by, for example, appropriate use of synonyms.

▶ Using finance-related terminology.

▶ Systematic checking of your work for errors and inaccuracies, particularly:

  – spelling errors

  – correct verb tenses

  – singular/plural agreements of nouns with verbs

  – correct use of definite and indefinite articles ('the' and 'a').

- ▶ Punctuating **properly.**
- ▶ **Being aware of** formal and informal styles.

There are opportunities to practise these points later in this Workbook.

Get help

You'll find it useful to have as many sources of help as possible as you practise writing, and in the run-up to the test.

- ▶ **Obtain a monolingual** English dictionary **to clarify the meaning of words you want to use when writing for practice.** *Note you are* NOT *allowed a dictionary in the exam*.

- ▶ **Obtain an** English grammar book **and use it if necessary when writing to improve your knowledge of language structure.** *Note you are* NOT *allowed a grammar book in the exam*.

- ▶ **Identify and memorise** opening and closing phrases.

- ▶ **Draw up a list of** connecting words and phrases. **Note which of them are used for** linking **similar ideas and which are used to** contrast **ideas.**

- ▶ **Build up your own list of** relevant financial English vocabulary **and make sure that you can spell each word correctly. When you record new words and phrases, always note whether they are best used in** formal **or relatively informal writing. Identify words that are** synonyms.

You have opportunities to develop these aids later in this Workbook.

In building up your vocabulary of relevant financial English you should be aware that finance-related areas which may come up in the test include the following.

► Financial reporting	► Company financial strategy
► Risk assessment and analysis	► Auditing
► Ethics and professionalism	► Accounting software packages
► Assets and company valuations	► Budgetary processes
► Corporate governance	► Cost and management accounting
► Environmental and sustainability issues	► Mergers and acquisitions
► Taxation (non-jurisdiction specific)	► Raising capital
► Insurance	► Banking and loan applications
► Investment banking	► Professional practice
► The stock market	► Foreign exchange and currency
► Debt-recovery and credit policy	► Bankruptcy and insolvency
► Forensic accounting	► Economic conditions and forecasts
► Pricing and purchasing	

Become familiar with the test

Make sure you are aware:

▶ of the standard format of the Writing paper, the instructions on the front page of the question paper, and the rubrics for each Part of the test.

▶ that you must write your answers in the test booklet itself, which is restricted in terms of space.

Develop a strategy for the test

Decide the following points in advance of the test on the basis of practice using this Workbook.

▶ The time you'll allocate to each Part (remember that Part 2 is worth 60% of the marks, Part 1 only 40%) and the word length. You should:

 – spend 30 minutes on the letter – and you should only write between 120 and 180 words

 – spend 45 minutes on the report – and you should only write between 200 and 250 words.

▶ The order in which you'll attempt the Parts. You may prefer to do the one you find easier first.

Be aware of how you will be assessed

Your answers are assessed with reference to two mark schemes:

▶ The General Mark Scheme is based on the examiner's overall impression, summarising the accuracy of language, including spelling and punctuation, the answer's content, organisation and cohesion, its range of structures and vocabulary, its tone and layout, and the target reader indicated in the task.

▶ The Task-Specific Mark Scheme Is based on the requirements of the particular task. You are penalised for dealing inadequately with these requirements.

▶ Spelling and punctuation are important aspects of accuracy and are always taken into account, though they are only penalized if errors impede impression or understanding (impeding errors). British and American spellings are equally valid, but you should be consistent.

▶ If handwriting interferes with communication without preventing it, the candidate will be penalized. Totally illegible scripts receive the lowest grade.

▶ The examiners' first priority is to give credit for your efforts at communication, but you are penalized for content that is irrelevant to the task set.

General Mark Scheme for Writing

The following bands of marks are available for the General Mark Scheme in the writing tasks:

Band	Level of performance
6	The task set is fully realized and the ideas are relevant and well developed. Ideas are logically organised and a wide range of vocabulary and complex structures is used effectively. Style and tone are consistently appropriate. There would be a very positive effect on the target reader.
5	There is good realization of the task set and the main ideas are relevant and developed. Ideas are logically organized and a good range of vocabulary and structures is used accurately. Style and tone are, on the whole, appropriate. There would be a positive effect on the target reader.
4	There is reasonable realization of the task set and the main ideas are relevant with some development. Ideas are generally logically organized and a reasonable range of vocabulary is used. There may, however, be some non-impeding errors in spelling and/or word formation. Style and tone are reasonably appropriate. Simple and complex structures are used but flexibility may be limited. It would achieve the desired effect on the target reader.
3	There is an adequate realization of the task set and the main ideas are relevant but some may lack clarity. Ideas are generally logically organized and an adequate range of vocabulary is used but word choice may lack precision in places. There is an adequate range of structures used, although errors in grammar occur and may cause difficulty for the reader. Style and tone may be inconsistent/inappropriate. It would, on the whole, achieve the desired effect on the target reader.
2	The task is not adequately addressed and, while there is evidence of organization, it is not wholly logical. The range of vocabulary is limited but minimally adequate for the task. The range of structures is limited and at times repetitive. Style and tone are often inconsistent/inappropriate. There would be a negative effect on the target reader.
1	The attempt at the task is poor and ideas are not organized coherently. The range of vocabulary is inadequate for or unrelated to the task and the range of structures is very limited. Style and tone are inappropriate for the task. There would be a very negative effect on the target reader.
0	The attempt achieves nothing and there is too little language for assessment or it is totally irrelevant or totally illegible.

Introduction to the letter task

What do I have to do?

Reply to a letter (the 'input letter') written to you in your role as an accountant, for instance by a client, plus five notes accompanying the letter. At least some of the notes mean your letter needs to cover finance-related issues relevant to the context of the task.

The overall aims of your letter are to communicate clearly to and have a positive effect on the target reader.

How many marks are there?

40% of the marks available for the exam.

How do I know what to 'say' in the letter?

What your letter needs to 'say' and to whom it needs to say it are dependent on four key things:

▶ the input letter with which you are presented in the task,

▶ the notes appended to the input letter,

▶ the function(s) of your letter as specified in the rubric, and

▶ the target reader.

What might the letter's function be?

You must cover the function(s) specified in the rubric so that the target reader is fully informed. You should prepare yourself for the letter's function being any one of the following (or a combination of these):

▶ Expressing opinions

▶ Explaining

▶ Disagreeing

▶ Persuading

▶ Presenting arguments

▶ Evaluating options

▶ Summarizing

▶ Apologizing

▶ Describing

▶ Advising

▶ Giving reasons

▶ Suggesting/proposing solutions or next steps

▶ Justifying decisions

▶ Hypothesizing

▶ Prioritizing

▶ Comparing and contrasting

▶ Correcting

▶ Recommending

What should I include in the letter?

As a minimum your letter should follow the usual conventions of letter writing, specifically:

- an opening salutation (Dear...)
- clear paragraphing, and
- a closing phrasing (yours faithfully/sincerely...)

You don't need to include postal addresses, though you won't be penalized if you do.

What is being tested by the letter task?

The examiner is looking for:

- successful communication
- clear and appropriate layout
- concise expression
- controlled and accurate language
- a range of complex language (you will get credit for the attempt even if you make mistakes, as long as these don't impede communication)
- appropriate style and tone
- well-organized and balanced content
- cohesion
- appropriate addressing of finance-related issues.

How should I approach the letter task?

▶ Read all of the input material carefully, especially the opening paragraphs, the five notes and the rubric's instructions.

▶ Highlight key words in the input letter (rather than lifting whole segments from the input you need to build on these key words to show your range of language).

▶ Number the five notes so you don't lose track.

▶ Think carefully about: your role; the target reader; the finance-related area being dealt with; the function of your letter; what layout, style and tone are appropriate.

▶ Plan how, in your letter, you will address each of the five notes.

▶ Identify which of the five notes you will expand on, and which will require a comparatively brief treatment.

▶ Write your letter concisely, using a range of complex language, and making sure that you cover each of the five notes to the right level in a separate paragraph.

▶ Check that you have covered all five notes, and check for errors.

How will my letter be assessed?

Your letter will be assessed with reference to the General Mark Scheme, as set out on page 104 of this Workbook, and the Task-Specific Mark Scheme that the marker will use for each specific task.

How should I prepare for the letter task?

▶ Read through the guidance on how to gear function, style and tone to the target reader, the example and then the guidance on getting started, on writing concisely and on checking for errors.

▶ Follow the guidance on practice on page 100 of this Workbook.

▶ When completing the Full Practice Tasks on page 129, follow the approach set out above.

▶ Practise using your own words when incorporating information from the input letter.

▶ Practise turning note forms into full sentences, paying particular attention to verb tenses, singular/plural agreements of nouns with verbs and use of definite/indefinite articles.

▶ Practise using a variety of connecting words to link the content in your letter.

How do I gear function, style and tone to my target reader?

The nature of the writing exam means that you'll always have to use formal expressions, but the target reader and the function of the letter may indicate the degree of formality.

The target reader may be:	So the function of the letter will be:	So the appropriate style and tone are:
A client with a complaint	To acknowledge the complaint, apologize and indicate how the problem is being resolved	Style: relatively formal Tone: polite, apologetic and helpful
A colleague with a query	To acknowledge the query and answer it, or explain why it cannot be answered	Style: relatively informal Tone: polite, friendly and direct
A supplier demanding payment	To acknowledge the demand and indicate the action you'll take	Style: relatively formal Tone: polite but neutral
A client contact seeking information from you as the client's adviser	To acknowledge the request and supply the information, or explain why it cannot be supplied	Style: formal Tone: brief and polite
A manager making a decision	To identify the decision to be made and to persuade the manager as to what it should be	Style: relatively formal Tone: polite, clear and enthusiastic

Writing the letter – Example

You work for a firm of accountants. One of your clients, PDT Construction, has applied for a loan to purchase and develop an industrial site. You have received the following letter from PDT Construction's bank.

Read the letter from Lars Fleming, an Account Manager at the bank, on which you have already made some notes (1 to 5). Then, using all the information in your notes, write to the bank on behalf of your client, PDT Construction.

We have recently received a loan application to purchase an industrial site from a mutual client, PDT Construction. However, before we can process the application, we require further information on some points.

Firstly, in the breakdown of costs for the project we cannot find any reference to architects' fees. Can you explain this? *1 Will use in-house staff*

In addition, although we requested company figures for the last five years we have only received accounts for the past four years. Why is this? *2 Give reason*

The funding for the project is also not clear to us. PDT Construction have requested a loan from this bank for only 65% of the total investment. We need to know where the remaining 35% will come from. *3 Explain*

Finally, a representative from our bank has looked at the site and the bank is concerned that the purchase price for the site may be too high. *4 Disagree – say why*

I look forward to hearing from you. *5 Suggest a meeting to discuss*

Yours sincerely,

Lars Fleming

Account Manager

Write a letter of between 120 and 180 words in an appropriate style on the following page. Do not write any postal addresses.

(Sample paper)

*The numbering on the notes should be added by you; on the exam paper there will be no numbering.

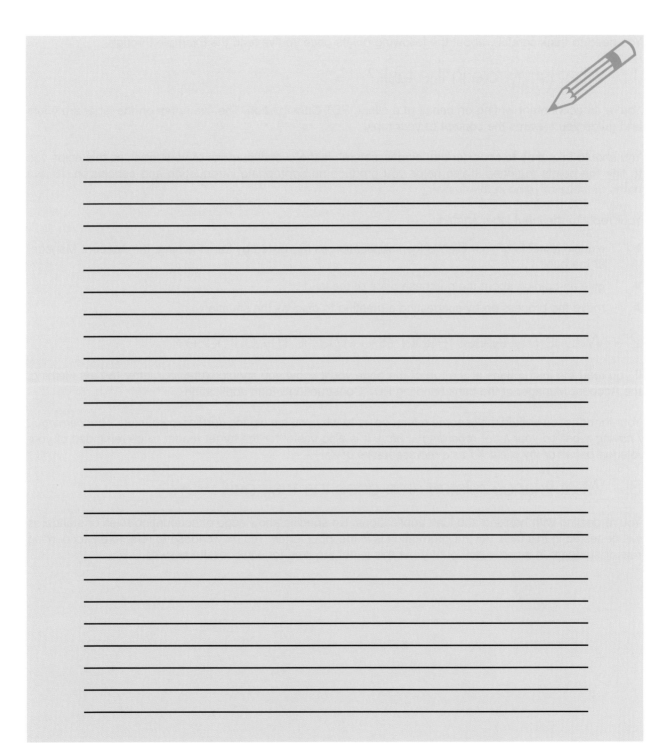

Getting started on the letter task

You need to think carefully about the following points once you've read the Example through.

1   What is my role in the task?

You're an accountant writing on behalf of a client, PDT Construction. The five notes on the letter are yours and guide you towards the content of your reply.

You should take time to consider the 'bigger picture', ie the overall purpose of your letter, as this helps you to link the points together. It also helps you produce an appropriate introduction and conclusion. All five notes must be covered in the answer.

Your reply to the input letter should:

▶   explain aspects of your client's loan application as requested by Lars Fleming, the Account Manager at the bank

▶   give an opinion about the purchase price of the land

▶   move the process on by suggesting a meeting to discuss the situation

2   Who is my target reader and what is my purpose?

If you read the instructions at the top of the page you'll know you should write your letter to Lars Fleming, the Account Manager at the bank handling PDT Construction's loan application.

Your introduction should make some reference as to why you are writing *(further to your letter concerning ... / having received your letter regarding ... etc.)*. It is also useful for the target reader to be reminded of your role *(on behalf of my client X / as a representative of X)*.

3   What finance-related area does the task deal with?

You're dealing with banking and loan applications. No specific knowledge of accounting rules or standards will be tested in this task. All the information is in the input letter. You may choose to refer to an accounting rule or standard in a particular country but this is not required for a successful answer.

4   What language functions are needed to complete the task?

Each note in the input letter must be addressed, and in doing so you'll be using a range of language functions.

▶   Explaining (Note 1: in-house staff will be used so there are no architects' fees in project costs)

▶   Giving a reason (Note 2: a plausible reason why only four years' accounts have been submitted)

▶   Explaining (Note 3: a plausible explanation of where the 35% balance of the total investment will come from)

▶   Disagreeing and explaining (Note 4: a plausible explanation of why the purchase price of the site is not too high)

▶   Suggesting next steps (Note 5: a meeting)

You don't have to expand each point equally. It may be appropriate to expand some points more than others eg explaining a point may need more development than suggesting a meeting.

5   What style and tone are appropriate?

The letter is from an accountant (you) to a fellow professional (a bank official) and needs to be in a formal and neutral tone. The notes on the input letter may, in some tasks, be informal and then you'll need to adopt this style when addressing the notes in the reply. Refer back to page 108 for guidance on how to gear style and tone to the target reader.

The Part 1 task is always a letter written by you in the role of accountant, so it will always need to be written in a comparatively formal style.

We look at the model answer for the Example later in this Workbook. First you should attempt the following Practice Exercises.

Practice Exercises for the Letter

1   Practice exercise on formal expressions

For each of the informal phrases below, identify a more formal alternative phrasing that would be appropriate in your letter.

Informal phrase	Formal alternative
Just got your letter and thought I'd let you know what I think!	
Here's the information you wanted.	
Looks like we've got a problem here!	
Things have gone pretty badly on the project.	
If you could get back to me, that'd be great.	
Hope to hear from you asap.	

How can I write more concisely?

You are writing concisely if:

▶   You write a message in as few words as possible.

▶   You are aware that every word counts.

▶   You avoid unnecessary explanations.

▶   You are clear and specific.

2 Practice exercise on writing concisely I

Replace the underlined sections of the following answer to the Example with more concise expressions so that the answer is closer to the word limit (120 – 180 words).

Dear Mr Fleming

Thank you for your letter <u>in regard to</u> the <u>subject of our client, PDT Construction, and their application for a loan</u>. Please find below <u>our clarifications and explanations for</u> the issues <u>which you raised</u> in your letter.

<u>Among the hundred employees currently working for PDT Construction, there are ten architects working</u>. They <u>possess qualified certificates in architect field and are well experienced</u>. They <u>will be responsible</u> for the design of the industrial site. Therefore the architects' fees will not be charged for this project.

PDT Construction was founded in <u>the October of 2000</u>. It was decided by the management board <u>to set the</u> accounting period <u>to start at January 1st and end at 31st December</u>. As a result, the financial statement of 2000 only covered 3 months of operation and <u>as such</u> does not reflect <u>in an accurate way</u> the company's activities.

PDT Construction has applied for 65% of the total investment. <u>As you know, it is planned that the project will be financed 65% by your bank</u>. The remaining 35% of <u>the funding for the project</u> will be generated from our profit reserves earned in the last <u>3 years we have operated</u>.

I would like to assure you that the <u>price currently being asked for</u> the site is not too high. If you look at the <u>strategic plan where all the details are explained</u>, you <u>will have to see the future potential of this location and then you will accept that the price is a good reflection of this</u>.

We would like to suggest <u>a meeting</u> next week at a time <u>that is</u> convenient to you.

Yours sincerely

272 words

3　Practice exercise on writing concisely II

From the unamended answer on page 115, identify a specific example of each of the following ways of lacking conciseness, and identify how each example could be written more concisely. We have completed the first one for you.

	Not concise	Concise
Using more words than you need to	'our clarifications and explanations for the issues which you raised in your letter'	'our comments on the issues raised in your letter'
Not being aware that every word counts		
Explaining something unnecessarily		
Not being clear or specific		

How can I eradicate errors in my writing?

There are various ways in which errors can creep into your writing. You're not penalized for errors in spelling and punctuation so long as you are writing using a range of complex language. However errors can create a very bad impression and can ultimately get in the way of effective communication, at which point you'll be penalized.

The types of error that are most common are:

▶ Using the wrong verb tense, or being inconsistent with tenses

▶ Inaccurate spelling

▶ Getting word order wrong

▶ Using the wrong word

▶ Using the wrong phrase

▶ Failing to ensure singular/plural agreement of nouns and verbs

▶ Using the definite (the) and indefinite (a/an) articles inappropriately

4   Practice exercise on error-free writing

Use the table provided to work through this answer to the Example on page 110, identifying as many errors as possible.

Thanks a lot for your reply on the loan application by PDT Construction. I'd like to clarify the following issues:

Firstly, in the breakdown of costs for the project we not show the cost of architects' fees because we currently have in-house staff for this. Most of our staff has a lot of experience in this area. We like to escape being dependent on outside staff.

Secondly, we have not accounts for the last five years because our company have start up in the middle of 2002. In the year 2000, there is no busines.

Thirdly, we require only a loan of 65% of the total investment. You see from our accounts that profits have grown up. We will use our profits for the investment.

Finally, we understand that because some companies in the area have closed you think too high the purchase price. On the other hand, we think the price is right for the market.

I suggest a meeting to discuss these issues. You should not hasitate to contact me for more information.

Yours sincerely

Errors in answer:

Tense	Spelling	Word order	Wrong word	Wrong phrase	Other

To help you build your understanding of what is required to secure a good or excellent grade in this task, we shall look at four answers to the Example (the sample paper on page 110) and try some further Practice Exercises based on them. Be warned – the answers are of varying quality! The 'band' identified for each answer relates to the General Mark Scheme on page 104.

Band 1 answer: poor and badly organized

Dear Mr Fleming

As you got the letter from Lars Fleming account manager PDT's Construction, you somehow need some clarifications, so on behalf of Lars we give you further information.

The biggest problem lies with us is the breakdown of costs, as you want explaination its all because we will now use inhouse staff who can deal with the project and make sure there are no breakdown of costs.

Due to the inner-problem in our mainstream computers our accounts for fifth year were delayed, but in two weeks time we will show our company figures as our organisation is working on it.

The remaing 35% will come from the future insurance and the new plant bought forward by our company, its just a matter of time and patience.

No, that's absolutely wrong because if you see our past records, you will see we are gaining profit and have minimized loss as compared to others.

We can have a meeting if you have more questions I will make sure you are totally convinced and satisfied.

Yours

176 words

Examiner's comments

This is a poor attempt at the task. Three of the five content points are misunderstood and this, together with the very confusing opening paragraph, indicates that the candidate does not fully understand the scenario in the input letter and is not, therefore, able to use the information correctly. Although there is evidence of organisation and some use of linking devices, there are errors in word choice and punctuation making the content difficult to follow in places. The style and tone are generally too informal.

5 Practice exercise on the Band 1 answer: misunderstanding the task

Explain which three of the five content points were misunderstood.

Band 3 answer: adequate but awkward

Dear Mr Fleming

Thank you for your letter requesting us some additional information on the loan application.

We can say that the breakdown of cost does not consist any architects' fees as we are going to use our highly-qualified in-house staff in the project.

We have not provided you with our accounts for the first year because our company was just established only four years ago and the figures of the balance sheet for four years will show you the objective picture.

We are going to invest in this project our own money in the amount of 35% of the total investment that is why we have requested a loan for only 65%.

We are sure that the purchase price for the site is not too high as it was prooved by the repot of a wellknown appraisal company.

To discuss these and any other details we can organise a meeting with a representative of PDT Construction next week.

If you need any further information please do not hesitate to contact us.

Best regards

174 words

Examiner's comments

This is an adequate attempt at the task. All the content points are included although with some awkwardness in places. The letter is well organized with suitable paragraphing and some use of simple cohesive devices. The range of vocabulary is adequate but sometimes the word choice lacks precision. The style and tone is generally appropriate and the letter contains some good formal expressions. The range of structures is adequate although there is some repetition; there are a few errors in spelling and punctuation but these are non-impeding.

6   Practice Exercise on the Band 3 answer: awkwardness and imprecision

Try to identify at least four examples of what the examiner refers to as 'awkwardness' and 'imprecision' in this answer.

Band 5 answer: good but incomplete

Dear Mr Fleming

In reply to your letter dated 14 June regarding the loan application of our mutual client, PDT Construction, we would like to comment as follows.

Firstly, our loan application does not show any architects' fees as you expected in the breakdown of costs for the project. Please note that PDT Construction plans to use in-house staff for architecture work. Therefore, the costs have been included in the operational costs of the project.

We also understand that your bank requires company figures for the last five years. However, PDT Construction has been operating only since 2001. As such, we are unable to provide company figures prior to that year.

The company has requested a loan for only 65% of the total investment as the remaining 35% of the fund is financed by retained profit from the last two years. Please refer to the financial statements for more information.

Your bank's assessment of the purchase price is different from ours. We have done a valuation on the site with support from a third party and enclose the valuation report for your reference.

We hope the above is clear. Please contact us if you need any clarification.

Yours sincerely

199 words

Examiner's comments

This is a good, confident letter which develops the information in the task extremely well although, unfortunately, the final note (suggesting a meeting) is omitted. The letter is well organized with suitable paragraphing and a range of cohesive devices is used. There is a very good range of vocabulary and effective use of financial expressions. The style and content is consistently formal and the control of complex structures is good. The task penalty concerning the final note holds this answer in Band 5, however.

7 Practice exercise on the Band 5 answer: conciseness I

At 199 words this answer is a little long (though not long enough to attract a penalty). Identify two sentences that could be written more concisely.

Band 6 answer: full realization

Dear Mr Fleming

In response to your enquiry regarding the loan application of our mutual client, PDT Construction, we are pleased to provide the following details.

Firstly, our client intends to use in-house architects for any work required for the project in question at no incremental costs that could be traced to this particular project.

Secondly, the set of accounts for the most recent accounting period has not yet been signed off by the client's Board. This delay is due to our client's accounting and reporting system to IFRS, requiring additional valuation of our client's fixed assets. To accommodate your need to access these figures, we have obtained their permission to release the latest management accounts and these are enclosed.

Thirdly, our client restructured their portfolio during the first half of the accounting period just ended. The resulting disposal of assets (see Note 16 of the management accounts enclosed) at unexpectedly high prices allowed our client to accumulate sufficient cash reserves to finance the remaining 35% of the total investment.

Despite the recent surge in property prices, this particular site has been significantly undervalued. We enclose a copy of the most recent valuation report for your reference.

We are open to any further discussion and ready to meet you in person to clarify any of these or additional details.

Yours sincerely

221 words

Examiner's comments

This is a full realization of the task showing confident use of language in developing all the notes very well. The letter is effectively organized and a wide range of vocabulary is used, including appropriate financial expressions and terminology. The letter is written in a consistently businesslike tone and a wide range of complex structures is employed. There are occasional inaccuracies in word choice but generally this response displays a high degree of accuracy and would have a very positive effect on the target reader.

8 Practice exercise on the Band 6 answer: conciseness II

At 221 words this answer is long, though again not long enough to attract a penalty. Identify two areas where less explanation could have been given without undermining the sense or impression of the answer.

Answers to Practice Exercises

Answer to practice exercise 1 on formal expressions

Informal phrase	Formal alternative
Just got your letter and thought I'd let you know what I think!	Thank you for your letter of 19 June 20XX. In response to your queries I would make the following points.
Here's the information you wanted.	We can provide you with the following information.
Looks like we've got a problem here!	There are certainly some key issues that require attention.
Things have gone pretty badly on the project.	There are certainly some key issues that require attention.
If you could get back to me, that'd be great.	I look forward to your prompt reply.
Hope to hear from you asap.	I look forward to your prompt reply.

Dear Mr Fleming,

Thank you for your letter regarding the loan application of our client, PDT Construction. Please find below our comments on the issues raised in your letter.

There are ten fully qualified and experienced architects among the hundred employees currently working for PDT Construction. They are responsible for the design of the industrial site and therefore architects' fees will not be charged to this project.

PDT Construction was founded in October 2000. It was decided by the management board that the accounting period would run from 1 January until 31 December. As a result, the financial statement for 2000 only covered 3 months of operation, which does not reflect accurately the company's activities.

PDT Construction has applied for 65% of the total investment. The remaining 35% of the funding will be generated from our profit reserves earned in the last 3 operating years.

I would like to assure you that the current price of the site is not too high. If you look at the details of the strategic plan for this location, you will see that the price accurately reflects the site's potential.

We would like to suggest meeting next week at a time convenient to you.

Yours sincerely

202 words

Answer to practice exercise 3 on writing concisely II

	Not concise	Concise
Using more words than you need to	'our clarifications and explanations for the issues which you raised in your letter'	'our comments on the issues raised in your letter'
Not being aware that every word counts	'in the October of 2000'	'in October 2000'
Explaining something unnecessarily	'As you know, it is planned the project will be financed 65% by your bank.'	- (they already know this)
Not being clear or specific	'will have to see the future potential of this site and then you will accept that the price is a good reflection of this'	'you will see that the price accurately reflects the site's potential'

Answer to practice exercise 4 on error-free writing

You may have come up with the other errors, but here are the main ones.

Tense	Spelling	Word order	Wrong word	Wrong phrase	Other
'have start up' **started up**	'hasitate' **hesitate**	'you think to high the purchase price..' You think **the purchase price is too high**	'escape' **avoid**	'on the other hand' **however**	'our staff has' **our staff have** (singular/plural agreement)
in the year 2000, there is In the year 2000 there **was**	no busines no **business**	we require only a loan of 65% of we **only require** a loan of 65% of	profits have grown up profits **have grown**		reply on the loan application **reply to** the loan application
We have not accounts We **do not have** accounts					we not show the cost we **did not** show the cost

Answer to practice exercise 5 on the Band 1 answer

i   Note 1: the bank asked why there were no architects' fees in the breakdown or analysis of PDT's projected costs supplied by PDT to the bank. The candidate has misinterpreted the query as being to do with controlling project costs within certain parameters. The candidate has also misinterpreted the note therefore: this relates to PDT using their own staff to do the job of architects, whereas the candidate has assumed it means that PDT will use their own staff to control costs.

ii   The paragraph responding to Note 3 suggests a lack of understanding. 'Future insurance' and 'plant brought forward' do not really make sense as sources of funding.

iii   The response to Note 4 is completely inappropriate, as the input letter asked about the purchase price agreed for the site while the candidate's letter refers to PDT's overall results.

Answer to practice exercise 6 on the Band 3 answer

Paragraph 1:   It should read 'requesting from us'. In addition 'the loan application' alone is too imprecise; it should say something like 'the loan application of our client, PDT Construction'.

Paragraph 2:   It should read 'does not contain any architects' fees'.

Paragraph 3:   Having both 'just' and 'only' in one sentence is awkward. In addition it should read 'figures in the balance sheet'.

Paragraph 4:   The phrase 'our own money' should immediately follow 'invest'.

Paragraphs 2-5: Each of these paragraphs starts with 'we'. Repetition of such simple language structure creates an awkward impression.

Answer to practice exercise 7 on the Band 5 answer

'Firstly, our loan application does not show any architects' fees as you expected in the breakdown of costs for the project' is a sentence that repeats something the target reader already knows. It could be omitted.

'We also understand that your bank requires company figures for the last five years' is lifted from the input letter and adds nothing. It could be omitted.

Answer to practice exercise 8 on the Band 6 answer

The second and third points are very well-developed in the answer and could have been reduced without detracting from the overall quality.

Full Practice Task for the letter

You work for a firm of accountants. One of your clients, Greenberg Products, has contacted a venture capital firm, FWC, with a view to expanding its manufacturing side by building a new factory. You have received the following letter from FWC.

Read the letter from Gloria Kutsakova, a director of FWC, on which you have made some notes. Then, using all the information in your notes, write a letter to Ms Kutsakova on behalf of your client, Greenberg Products.

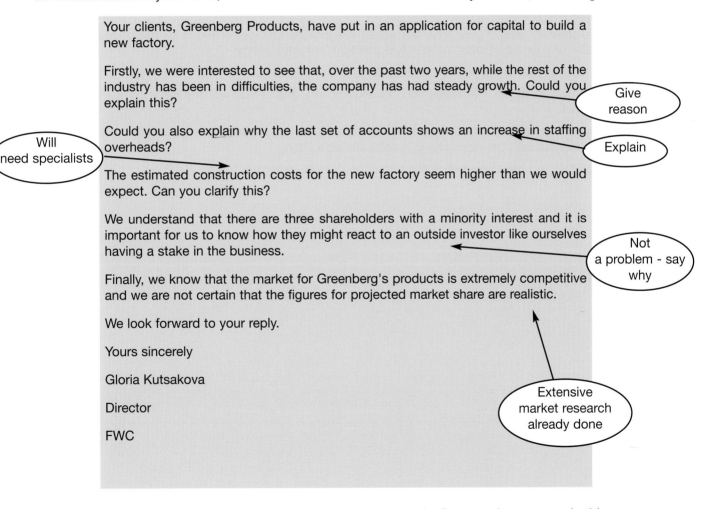

Your clients, Greenberg Products, have put in an application for capital to build a new factory.

Firstly, we were interested to see that, over the past two years, while the rest of the industry has been in difficulties, the company has had steady growth. Could you explain this?

Give reason

Could you also explain why the last set of accounts shows an increase in staffing overheads?

Explain

Will need specialists

The estimated construction costs for the new factory seem higher than we would expect. Can you clarify this?

We understand that there are three shareholders with a minority interest and it is important for us to know how they might react to an outside investor like ourselves having a stake in the business.

Not a problem - say why

Finally, we know that the market for Greenberg's products is extremely competitive and we are not certain that the figures for projected market share are realistic.

Extensive market research already done

We look forward to your reply.

Yours sincerely

Gloria Kutsakova

Director

FWC

Write a letter of between 120 and 180 words in an appropriate style. Do not write any postal addresses.

(You would be given one lined page to write your answer.)

(May 2007 Paper)

Remember you should follow the standard approach to the letter task:

▶ Read all of the input material carefully, especially the opening paragraphs, the five notes and the rubric's instructions.

▶ Highlight key words in the input so you can build on them to show your range of language.

▶ Number the five notes so you don't lose track.

▶ Think carefully about: your role; the target reader; the finance-related area being dealt with; the function of your letter; what layout, style and tone are appropriate.

▶ Plan how, in your letter, you will address each of the five notes.

▶ Identify which of the five notes you will expand on, and which will require a comparatively brief treatment.

▶ Write your letter concisely, using a range of complex language, and making sure that you cover each of the five notes to the right level in a separate paragraph.

▶ Check that you have covered all five notes, and check for errors.

Writing the letter – Answer to Full Practice Task

The annotated question paper below shows how the recommended standard approach has been followed in preparing the model answer. We have highlighted key points in the rubric and the input letter, numbered the five notes and identified those we should expand on and made notes as to what we shall say:

Annotated question

You work for a firm of accountants. One of your clients, Greenberg Products, has contacted a venture capital firm, FWC, with a view to expanding its manufacturing side by building a new factory. You have received the following letter from FWC.

Read the letter from Gloria Kutsakova, a director of FWC, on which you have made some notes. Then, using all the information in your notes, write a letter of between 120 and 180 words to Ms Kutsakova on behalf of your client, Greenberg Products.

Your clients, Greenberg Products, have put in an application for capital to build a new factory.

Firstly, we were interested to see that, over the **past two years, while the rest of the industry has been in difficulties, the company has had steady growth**. Could you explain this?

Could you also explain why the last set of accounts shows an **increase in staffing overheads**?

The **estimated construction costs** for the new factory seem higher than we would expect. Can you clarify this?

We understand that there are **three shareholders with a minority interest** and it is important for us to know how they might react to an outside investor like ourselves having a stake in the business.

Finally, we know that the market for Greenberg's products is **extremely competitive and we are not certain that the figures for projected market share are realistic.**

We look forward to your reply.

Yours sincerely

Gloria Kutsakova

Director

FWC

2 Explain
To enable new product & process innovation

3 Will need specialists so the factory is efficient

4 Not a problem - say why
Minority = founders/directors
Expand

1 Give reason
Innovation & quality in products & processes. Increased market share & wider margins
Expand

5 Extensive market research already done.
Link to strategy. Figures based on research

131

We have also identified answers to the following points:

Target reader: Director of company giving money to my client

Area: Raising capital

Function: 1 Give reasons; 2 & 4 Explain; 3 & 5 Clarify

Layout: Introduction; 5 paragraphs; sign-off

Style/tone: Formal

Model answer

Dear Ms Kutsakova

In response to your enquiry regarding the capital application from our client, Greenberg Products, I am pleased to provide the following details.

The company's steady growth results from its strategy of innovation and quality in both products and processes, leading to increased market share and wider margins. Competitors which have not followed such a strategy have indeed struggled over the past two years.

Last year's increase in staffing overheads reflects investment in highly qualified staff to drive new product development and improvements in quality.

To make it more efficient in operation the new factory will require the involvement of specialist designers and engineers in its construction, so the estimate of construction costs is relatively high.

Currently Greenberg Products' three directors are its only shareholders. Following your investment their shareholdings will be the minority interest. They are each committed to the company's expansion strategy and FWC's involvement.

Extensive market research indicates that the strategy of innovation, quality and expansion will be successful in a competitive market. The figures for projected market share are based on this research.

Please do not hesitate to contact me if you require further clarification.

Yours sincerely

192 words

Introduction to the report task

What do I have to do?

Read a relatively brief context with four content points, and then write a 200 – 250 word report with a specific purpose for a target reader. You may have to write to a client, to a colleague/fellow accountant or to a senior professional. All four content points must be addressed. You'll be expected to develop finance-related topics and discuss finance-related issues in your report.

The overall aims of your report are to communicate clearly to and have a positive effect on the target reader.

How many marks are there?

60% of the marks available for the exam.

How do I know what to 'say' in the report?

What your report needs to 'say' and to whom it needs to say it are dependent on four key things:

▶   the context
▶   the purpose for the report
▶   the target reader and
▶   four content points

As well as addressing all four content points you must also produce a well-balanced report. The points don't necessarily need equal amounts of writing. Watch out in particular for clues in the context as to whether, for example, you need only consider something briefly.

Warning!

Don't try to reproduce a report you've done before on a similar topic as such answers rarely address the task set. You've got to address the key things listed above, not simply write 250 words on the topic.

What might the report's purpose be?

You must cover the report's purpose as specified so that the target reader is fully informed. You should prepare yourself for the report's purpose being any one of the following (or a combination of these):

▶ Evaluating ideas

▶ Presenting and developing arguments

▶ Expressing and supporting opinions

▶ Describing

▶ Summarizing

▶ Recommending

▶ Persuading

▶ Explaining

What should I include in the report?

As a minimum your report should follow the usual conventions of report writing, specifically:

▶ an introduction

▶ clear paragraphing (ideally with brief headings)

▶ a conclusion if required by the content points

What is being tested by the report task?

In testing your ability to produce a report the examiner is looking for:

▶ successful communication

▶ appropriate style and tone

▶ range of vocabulary

▶ range of structure

▶ grammatical accuracy

- ▶ a range of complex language (you'll get credit for the attempt even if you make mistakes, as long as these don't impede communication)
- ▶ development of finance-related topics and discussion of finance-related issues in a non-technical way

How should I approach the report task?

- ▶ Read all of the input material carefully, especially the context, the purpose, the target reader and the content points.
- ▶ Highlight key words in the input material (rather than lifting whole segments from the input you need to build on these key words to show your range of language).
- ▶ Number the content points so you don't lose track, and check whether there is more than one part to each one.
- ▶ Think carefully about: your role; the target reader; the finance-related area being dealt with; the purpose of your report; what layout, style and tone are appropriate.
- ▶ Plan how, in your report, you will address each of the content points appropriately within the word limit (200 – 250 words).
- ▶ Identify whether any of the content points require either expansion or a relatively brief treatment
- ▶ Consider what knowledge can be assumed and what should be included, and to what extent factual points need illustration.
- ▶ Write your report concisely, using a range of complex language, and making sure that you cover each of the four content points to the right level in a separate paragraph with a heading.
- ▶ Check that you have covered all the four content points, and check for errors.

How will my report be assessed?

Your report will be assessed with reference to the General Mark Scheme, as set out on page 104 of this Workbook, and the Task-Specific Mark Scheme.

How should I prepare for the report task?

Make sure that you have followed the example for the letter thoroughly before commencing your preparation for the report.

Writing the report – Example

You work for an accountancy firm and one of your clients is a small airline. This airline is considering purchasing a new aircraft within the next twelve months to expand its operations. The airline has asked your firm for advice concerning this purchase and you have considered the airline's financial position.

Write a **report** for the airline. Your report should:

▶ explain which internal financial indicators most accurately show the financial position of this airline

▶ summarize the airline's current financial position

▶ outline what risks there would be in expansion

▶ advise the airline on what steps to take next.

Write your report in **200 – 250** words in an appropriate style.

(You would be given two lined pages on which to write your answer.)

(Sample paper)

Getting started on the report task

You need to think carefully about the following questions once you've read the Example through.

1 What is my role in the task?

You're an accountant writing to a client (an airline) to advise on a proposed expansion of its operations via the purchase of one new aircraft. The four content points provide the structure of your report. You'll need to invent some information to fit into the structure of the answer, eg the airline's current financial position. You must cover all four content points in your report.

2 Who is my target reader and what is my purpose?

You should write your report to the client airline in line with the context as explained at the start of the question. Your introduction should make reference to its purpose (eg *The purpose of this report is to … This report addresses the issue of …*) and in the conclusion you should make a recommendation as to the next steps (this is one of the content points). It's realistic as well, though not obligatory, to offer further support (eg *We remain at your disposal for… Do not hesitate to contact us if …*).

3 What finance-related area does the task deal with?

You're dealing with company financial strategy. You're expected to be familiar with core finance-related areas from your course and/or work and you should therefore be able to identify some internal financial indicators and discuss in broad terms a company's financial position. However, what you're assessed on is the way in which you develop your ideas. Specific accountancy knowledge is not assessed.

4 What language functions are needed to complete the task?

You need to read the content points very carefully to establish the language functions. While you must address each content point in your report it's not necessary to expand each point equally: you can expand some points more than others.

Your report should:

- explain which financial indicators show the client's financial position – so ideally you would cover why particular financial indicators are useful as well as simply stating which ones are useful
- summarize the client's current financial position – this should be comparatively brief, but should be backed up with 'factual' information (which you have to make up!)
- outline the risks in expansion – so again this should be comparatively brief
- advise on next steps – as with explaining, the function of advising requires more depth

5   What style and tone are appropriate?

Your report is from an accountant to a client and needs to be in a neutral or formal style and tone. The content of the report must be clear to the target reader. Refer back to page 108 for guidance on how to gear style and tone to the target reader.

The task is always a report written by you as a professional, so it will always need to be written in a neutral or formal style and tone.

6   How do I tackle the content points?

For the report task, make brief notes on as many ideas for each of the content points as possible, including suitable words and phrases you would like to use. You can use bullet points in your answer but make sure these are fully formed sentences, not just lists of words.

We will look at the model answer for this Example later in this Workbook. First you should attempt the Practice Exercises that follow.

Practice Exercises for the report

1 Practice exercise on opening and closing expressions

a   Decide which of the following expressions should come at the opening (O) or closing (C) of a report.

b   In the list there are three expressions which are too informal for writing in a finance context. Identify these three expressions.

	Expression	O	C	Too informal?
1	Further to your request, I am pleased to provide the following details:			
2	I hope the above points clarify your concerns.			
3	I refer to my client's loan application.			
4	The following is an outline of my client's financial position.			
5	I look forward to an early reply.			
6	You should take into consideration the above mentioned points.			
7	This is in response to your request for a meeting to discuss the issue.			
8	Hope to hear from you asap.			
9	Please let me know if I can be of further assistance.			
10	I am writing on behalf of my client, Alpha Trading.			
11	If you could get back to me, that'd be great.			
12	To avoid further losses, I recommend the following action:			
13	I just got your letter and everything seems fine.			
14	Do not hesitate to contact me for further information.			
15	Our aim is to provide you with the relevant information.			
16	The purpose of this report is to advise on your proposed takeover.			
17	This report addresses the issue of performance measurement in your A Division			
18	We remain at your disposal for further advice if you require it.			
19	Do not hesitate to contact us if you require further information.			

How should I structure my report?

Your report needs a clear structure, including an introduction and a conclusion, either or both of which may be one of your four content points. Your report's structure is dictated by the fact that you need to cover each of the four content points. In total it should therefore contain between four and six paragraphs, depending on whether the introduction and/or conclusion are part of the content points.

2 Practice exercise on using paragraphs

Read the answer below and organize it into the following paragraphs:

1	Introduction
2	The relevant financial indicators
3	The company's current financial position
4	The risks involved in expansion
5	The next steps to take
6	Conclusion

Investment in a new aircraft requires the analysis of various factors influencing both the airline itself and the industry as a whole. Useful internal financial indicators include profitability ratios, especially the capital utilization ratio (ROCE) and retained earnings figures, and liquidity ratios. These help us to identify whether the company has the resources now and in the future to sustain its expansion. The company's ROCE is 15%, above average in the sector. Its current liquidity ratio is 1.5, which places the company in a good bargaining position when negotiating long-term loans. The airline could face problems in an industry which is very competitive. A new aircraft means more services and also increased maintenance costs and fuel. The airline staff must be able to cope with this increased workload. The risks are substantial since, besides the financial investment in an aircraft, the airline may need increased staff. This report is an advisory one. The next steps in decision making should take these points into consideration and should also assess the economic climate in which the airline is operating. The airline must consider how it plans to finance this expansion as, although a loan could be appropriate, the interest charges and other costs could be a burden on its financial affairs.

How do I turn my notes on the content points into full sentences?

In your planning process, when you are making notes on each of the content points your objects are:

▶   to think of as many ideas as possible, and

▶   to get them down on paper as quickly as possible, then

▶   to identify the ones you want to use, then

▶   to include the ideas in your report in the form of full sentences.

When looked at in this way, the process can seem rather daunting. The key is to make proper notes to begin with:

▶   Keep them short

▶   Express them clearly

▶   Identify them with phrases that you think will impress the examiner.

3 Practice exercise on turning notes into full sentences

For the content point below, make three notes for (i) ideas and (ii) related phrases to be included in your report, then work each into a full sentence.

Content point	Notes		Full sentence
	(i) Idea	(ii) Related phrase	
Explain which internal financial indicators most accurately show the financial position of this airline			

To help you build your understanding of what is required to secure a good or excellent grade in this task, we shall look at four answers to the Example (the sample paper) on page 136, and try some further Practice Exercises based on them. Be warned – they are of varying quality!

Band 2 answer: limited, too informal and with impeding errors

After the analysis basic on your requirement, we do some related explanation as follow.

According to your balance sheet, we found your assets is enough to afford the first period of expansion. But that's not enough to say you have the ability to expand. The current liability ratio, benifit to assets ratio and the cash flow index should be took into your consideration. The current liability ratio shows whether you can afford the payment, the benifit to assets ratio shows whether it's worth to do so and the cash flow index will add help to your decision. The special analysis data is on the attach paper. We want to say is just as long as the data you provide to us is true that you can expand.

In the expansion there are risks. Firstly you need to put more money on your advertisment fees which will decline your benifit. Secondly, even you do more advertisment your passages will not increase in that case you will face an empty plan. Thirdly, the added plan will carry which course will effect your current operation.

The strategy and your rival should also be took into account. You have to adjust your current strategy, to focus on more widely part to get more benifit. Meanwhile you should have a clear idea what your rivals have done to avoid clash.

If you do decide to expand, the first primary thing to do is decide how to use the new planes. You need a special plan of it and adjust your strategy corrently. Only when you do so, you can get the largest benefit from your expansion.

Hope your expansion will achieve a success result!

279 words

Examiner's comments

Although the main points in the question have been addressed and there is evidence of organization, this is not an adequate answer because the number of errors cause difficulty for the reader and the meaning is often unclear. There are frequent errors in word choice, some poor control of basic grammatical structures and repeated spelling errors. The range of structures is limited and at times repetitive. The tone of the report is often too informal and the ending is inappropriate.

4 Practice exercise on the Band 2 answer: error correction

The examiner highlights impeding errors as being one of this answer's problems. Identify how these five impeding errors could have been simply corrected by the writer when checking.

	Error	Correction
1	'assets is'	
2	'benifit'	
3	'should be took into your consideration'	
4	'advertisment'	
5	'corrently'	

On your previous request I am writing the summary report on the new aircraft purchase.

First of all, I would like to mention that your financial situation is considerable better than 6 months ago. All financial indicators (margins, assets, cash flow, return on capital employed, liabilities etc) appear to be at standard level. I can't see any issues to bring one more aircraft in your assets. We should get a loan covering 50% of value within 3 months. Then we will capitalise it as standard item.

Secondly we have to assume all risks on this decision. However your finance situation is good the competitors becoming stronger. You must be sure your aircraft is fully used and bring money immediately. I suggest to prepare a feasibility study just to make sure. You already know there will be a new policy about stricter technical controlls next year. And this will definitely bring additional costs. We have to assume the oil prices as well which are projected to be higher next year. According my calculation both these factors will increase the current costs by 11%.

Thirdly, I just recommend the next steps you should work on. Please, provide any relevant information that can assict your decision in buying new aircraft. Of course do not forget to make proper analysis – competitors, SWOT etc. These all will be a part for a loan request.

To sum up I can't see any difficulties from your financial position and if all non-financial aspects are considered then you can expand your business without worries.

You can find a financial analysis attached. There you can find all necessary performance indicators.

271 words

Examiner's comments

This is an adequate attempt at the task with all the necessary points included, although there is some lack of clarity in parts. The answer is suitably paragraphed but the use and control of cohesive devices is not always correct and confuses the reader at times. The range of vocabulary is adequate with some attempt to use financial terminology, although the word choice lacks precision at times. Sentence structure is mostly simple and there are some errors, mostly non-impeding however. The answer is generally too informal in tone and the ending is rather abrupt.

5   Practice exercise on the Band 3 answer: informality

The examiner highlights informality as being one of this answer's problems. Identify three different examples of informal language that impair this piece of writing, and state how each one could be changed.

	Type of informal language	Example	Change to
1			
2			
3			

Band 4 answer: adequate

Subject: Report on the factors that need to be considered before purchasing a new aircraft

In response to your request for advice on the factors to consider deciding to expand your operations by purchasing a new aircraft, we forward the following points.

In the first place, the company needs to assess the market conditions in which the company is going to expand its operations in. To this effect, it needs to carry out a thorough marketing study.

It should also look into its financial strength in terms of affording to purchase the aircraft including its capacity to win the willingness of financers to extend borrowings. To this effect you need to show the strength of your financial position by preparing analysis supported by financial indicators such as good quick and current ratios, good debt to equity ratios and also appealing return on assets ratios. From our experience, all these ratios in your accounts are in good shape to warrant obtaining fresh loan for the purchase of the aircrafts.

It is also necessary to look into the risks you might face:

▶ The management capabilities to handle an expanded business may become overstretched. Therefore you need to look into this now.

▶ Possible working capital problems may result from the expanssion of the business under capitalisation.

As a next step you need also to start looking for sources of finance i.e lenders and also to look into the legal and regulatory issues and requirements that may influence your decision.

Finally we would like to express our willingness to avail ourselves at your convenience to explain all the points in more detail.

270 words

Examiner's comments

This is a reasonable realization of the task. All the necessary points have been addressed and developed quite well in the report and it is well organised with effective use of simple cohesive devices and bullet points for clarity. There is an adequate range of vocabulary, including some appropriate financial terms, although there is also some repetition and awkwardness because of incorrect word choice. There are occasional lapses in style and tone and some errors, mainly non-impeding.

6 Practice exercise on the Band 4 answer: avoiding repetition and irrelevance

The examiner highlights repetition as being a slight problem in this answer.

a   Identify two instances of repetition and/or irrelevance in this piece of writing.

b   Indicate where the writer could have clarified the report by introducing another paragraph.

Band 6 answer: full realization

Cost benefit analysis of the company purchasing a new aircraft

The investment in a new aircraft requires the analysis of various factors influencing both the airline and the industry.

Financial position of the airline

The airline's current situation, based on its profitability and liquidity, must be secure. Useful internal financial indicators include the capital utilisation ratio (return on capital employed) and the retained earnings figure. The company's ROE (return on equity) is 15%, above average in the sector. The company's current liquidity ratio is 1.5 and places the company in a good bargaining position when negotiating long-term loans.

The risks of expansion

The airline could face problems in an industry which is very competitive. A new aircraft would mean more provision of services and also increased maintenance costs and fuel. The airline staff must be able to cope with the administration and servicing of an additional aircraft. The risks here are substantial since besides the financial investment in an aircraft, the airline may need increased staff for the new workload.

Next steps

This report is an advisory one. The next steps in decision making should take into consideration the above mentioned points and also assess the economic climate in which the airline is operating before investing in a new asset. The airline must consider the means of financing this expansion as, although a loan could be appropriate, the interest charges and other costs could be a burden on the financial affairs of the business.

244 words

Examiner's comments

This is a full realization of the task demonstrating confident use of language and effective control of complex structures. The points in the report are relevant and well developed. The report is organized logically with headings to ensure the information is conveyed clearly. There is a wide range of vocabulary including financial terms and generally good control of fixed phrases. The style and tone are consistently appropriate and this answer would have a very positive effect on the target reader.

Our comment

We think this answer would be even better if the second paragraph was split at 'retained earnings figure', so there was one paragraph covering internal financial indicators, and one covering the airline's current financial position.

Answers to Practice Exercises

Answer to practice exercise 1 on opening and closing expressions

See if you reached the same conclusions as us. As you encounter more opening and closing expressions during your studies or work, add them into the spaces provided below.

	Expression	O	C	Too informal?
1	Further to your request, I am pleased to provide the following details:	X		
2	I hope the above points clarify your concerns.		X	
3	I refer to my client's loan application.	X		
4	The following is an outline of my client's financial position.	X		
5	I look forward to an early reply.		X	
6	You should take into consideration the above mentioned points.		X	
7	This is in response to your request for a meeting to discuss the issue.	X		
8	Hope to hear from you asap.		X	X
9	Please let me know if I can be of further assistance.		X	
10	I am writing on behalf of my client, Alpha Trading.	X		
11	If you could get back to me, that'd be great.		X	X
12	To avoid further losses, I recommend the following action:		X	
13	I just got your letter and everything seems fine.	X		X
14	Do not hesitate to contact me for further information.		X	
15	Our aim is to provide you with the relevant information.	X		
16	The purpose of this report is to advise on your proposed takeover.	X		
17	This report addresses the issue of performance measurement in your A Division	X		
18	We remain at your disposal for further advice if you require it.		X	
19	Do not hesitate to contact us if you require further information.		X	

Answer to practice exercise 2 on using paragraphs

1	Introduction	Investment in a new aircraft requires the analysis of various factors influencing both the airline itself and the industry as a whole.
2	The relevant financial indicators	Useful internal financial indicators include profitability ratios, especially the capital utilization ratio (ROCE) and retained earnings figures, and liquidity ratios. These help us to identify whether the company has the resources now and in the future to sustain its expansion.
3	The company's current financial position	The company's ROCE is 15%, above average in the sector. Its current liquidity ratio is 1.5, which places the company in a good bargaining position when negotiating long-term loans.
4	The risks involved in expansion	The airline could face problems in an industry which is very competitive. A new aircraft means more services and also increased maintenance costs and fuel. The airline staff must be able to cope with this increased workload. The risks are substantial since, besides the financial investment in an aircraft, the airline may need increased staff.
5	The next steps to take	This report is an advisory one. The next steps in decision making should take these points into consideration and should also assess the economic climate in which the airline is operating.
6	Conclusion	The airline must consider how it plans to finance this expansion as, although a loan could be appropriate, the interest charges and other costs could be a burden on its financial affairs.

Answer to practice exercise 3 on turning notes into full sentences

Content point	Notes		Sentence
	Idea	Related phrase	
Explain which internal financial indicators most accurately show the financial position of this airline	Return on assets	Effective use of assets	**A return on assets** indicator such as ROCE identifies the airline's **effective use of assets** historicallly.
	Profitability	Wide margin	**Profitability** ratios show that the airline trades with a **wide margin** in comparison with the industry as a whole.
	Liquidity	Able to fund expansion	Your current and quick ratios indicate clearly that you have **liquidity** so you are **able to fund expansion** yourselves, at least in part.

Answer to practice exercise 4 on Band 2 answer

We have identified in our answer the nature of the error made, which highlights for you the things to watch out for when checking your work.

	Error	Correction	Nature of the error
1	'assets is'	assets **are**	Agreement of noun and verb
2	'benifit'	ben**efit**	Spelling
3	'should be took into your consideration'	should be **taken** into your consideration	Tense
4	'advertisment'	advertis**e**ment	Spellng
5	'corrently'	**cu**rrently	Spelling

Answer to practice exercise 5 on the Band 3 answer

1	Inappropriate abbreviation – 'I can't' should be 'I cannot'
2	Colloquial phrasing – 'just to make sure' should be 'to ensure usage will be sufficient'
3	Inappropriate phrase – 'of course do not forget to make proper analysis' should be 'I would remind you that proper analysis is important'

Answer to practice exercise 6 on the Band 4 answer

a 1 The subject header and the introduction not only repeat the same point, they actually repeat the same language ('purchasing a new aircraft'). No marks would be awarded for this so in effect the words are wasted and could have been omitted.

2 The second paragraph in the piece ('In the first place…') does not cover a content point and is therefore irrelevant.

b The third paragraph ('It should also look…') covers content points 1 and 2 and should therefore be paragraphed at 'From our experience…'

Full Practice Task for the report

(May 2007 Paper)

You work for an accountancy firm. One of your clients is setting up a new business, a retail company, and has asked for your advice on what to consider when purchasing accounting software.

Write a **report** for your client. Your report should:

▶ Outline the functions your retail client needs from an accounting software package

▶ Suggest what other factors it is important to consider before purchasing the software

▶ Describe what type of staff training may be necessary

▶ Say what help your firm can offer the client

Write your answer in **200-250** words in an appropriate style.

(You would be given two lined pages to write your answer).

Remember you should follow the standard approach to the report task as set out on page 135:

▶ Read all of the input material carefully, especially the context, the purpose, the target reader and the content points.

▶ Highlight key words in the input material (rather than lifting whole segments from the input you need to build on these key words to show your range of language).

▶ Number the content points so you don't lose track, and check whether there is more than one part to each one.

▶ Think carefully about: your role; the target reader; the finance-related area being dealt with; the purpose of your report; what layout, style and tone are appropriate.

▶ Plan how, in your report, you will address each of the content points appropriately within the word limit (200 – 250 words).

▶ Identify whether any of the content points require either expansion or a relatively brief treatment.

▶ Consider what knowledge can be assumed and what should be included, and to what extent factual points need illustration.

▶ Write your report concisely, using a range of complex language, and making sure that you cover each of the four content points to the right level in a separate paragraph with a heading.

▶ Check that you have covered all the four content points, and check for errors.

Writing the report – Answer to Full Practice Task

The annotated question paper below shows how the recommended standard approach has been followed in preparing the model answer. We have highlighted key words, numbered the four content points, identified the one we shall be briefed on and made notes as to what we shall say.

Context

You work for an accountancy firm. <u>One of your clients is setting up a new business, a retail company</u>, and has asked for <u>your advice on what to consider when purchasing accounting software</u>.

Target reader

Purpose

Write a **report** for your client. Your report should:

Content points

▶ 1   outline the **functions your retail client needs from an accounting software 2 package**

▶ 2   suggest what **other factors** it is important to consider before purchasing the software

▶ 3   describe what type of **staff training** may be necessary

▶ 4   say what **help your firm can offer** the client.

Write your answer in **200 – 250** words in an appropriate style.

We have also identified answers to the following points.

Target reader: Director of client setting up a retail company

Area: Accounting software packages

Purpose of report: 1: outline, 2: suggest, 3: describe, 4: suggest

Layout, style; tone: Intro + 4 paras + conclusion; formal + neutral

Finally, we have noted down the points to be made for each content point, and now this should be done briefly.

Content points

1   EPOS; stock control; purchase ledger; cash; branch accounting; ordering

2   Cost; reputation of seller; future development of software; future development of business; branches; feasibility study; security; compatibility

3   Staff training on: maintenance; use in shops (data entry); use in head office (all functions); producing reports; producing financial statements

4   Preparing brief; asking for tenders; selection process; implementation process; ongoing review; training

Model answer

Report on purchasing accounting software package

Further to your request for advice for your new retail company, we have pleasure in presenting the following matters for your consideration.

Functions of the accounting software package

As a retailer the company will require a range of functions to be performed. These will include, as a minimum, ordering and stock control functions, electronic funds transfer at point of sale capability, cash processing, purchase and nominal ledgers and a branch accounting facility.

Factors to consider before purchase

The costs of the software licence, and the installation and maintenance processes, are probably the most significant factors. You should also consider compatibility with existing systems and security. Looking to the future, any anticipated expansion must be capable of being supported by the chosen software. The supplier's reputation and stability should not be ignored. A feasibility study would establish fully the factors to be considered.

Staff training

Your staff will need to be trained to varying degrees in using the software. Shop staff need only receive basic training in data entry, while accounts staff will need full training in all functions. At least two people should be trained in maintenance and trouble shooting.

Assistance in the purchasing process

We would be happy to assist you with this key purchase. As your accountants we are well-placed to help you prepare a specification for potential suppliers. We can also support you in the tendering and selection processes, in implementation, and in ongoing review of the system. Our established training department can help with your staff training needs.

Please do not hesitate to contact us if you require further information.

270 words

Listening

Contents of the Listening section

Introduction to Listening

In this section you will:

▶ find out what you have to do in the ICFE Test of Listening
▶ focus on each part of the Test of Listening by looking at examples
▶ think about how to prepare yourself for the Test of Listening
▶ have a go at doing a Test of Listening

What do I have to do in the ICFE Test of Listening?

During the test you'll hear a range of different recordings set in a number of contexts related to a different aspect of finance and accounting.

The test will last for approximately 40 minutes, including five minutes at the end to transfer your answers to an answer sheet. On the answer sheet you will use a pencil to either shade in a box or write a word or words next to the corresponding question number.

There are 30 questions in the test.

What is in the ICFE Test of Listening?

The ICFE Test of Listening is divided into four parts.

Part 1

In this part you'll hear three short monologues or conversations. Each is about a minute long and there are two multiple-choice questions per recording, making six in total for this part. You'll hear each recording twice.

Part 2

In this part you'll hear a conversation between two or more speakers that lasts for about four minutes. There are five multiple-choice questions to answer as you listen and you'll hear the conversation twice.

Part 3

In this part you'll hear a monologue that will last for about four minutes. You'll have to complete the sentences on the question paper with a word or words that you hear on the recording. There are nine sentences to complete and you'll hear the recording twice.

Part 4

In this part you'll hear a series of five monologues all based on a particular theme. Each recording lasts for about 30 seconds and there are two matching tasks to complete for each, making a total of ten questions in this part. You'll hear all the monologues twice.

Listening Part 1

What do I have to do?

Listen to three short monologues or conversations and answer six questions, two questions per recording. For each pair of questions there is an introductory sentence written on the question paper and given in the recording that tells you who is talking and why or about what. You'll have 15 seconds before each recording to read through the two questions. The three recordings are not connected by theme and the questions are multiple choice, with three options, A-C. You'll need to think about all of the options carefully before deciding on your answer. The other options may appear possible, but only one will be completely correct in terms of the factual information you hear or the opinions and attitudes of the speakers. You will hear each recording twice.

What listening texts are used?

Short monologues such as announcements and briefings, and short dialogues such as meetings, discussions, interviews and consultations.

What is being tested?

Understanding gist, detail, function, purpose, topic, attitude, feeling, opinion and inference.

How many questions/marks are there?

6 questions for 6 marks – 1 mark each

How should I prepare for Part 1?

▶   Listen extensively to appropriate sources in order to become familiar with language spoken in a range of formal and less formal contexts.

▶   Pay attention to how people give their opinions and feelings and show agreement or disagreement.

▶   Practise using the 15 seconds before the recording starts to read the tasks quickly in order to know what you need to listen for.

Listening Part 1– Exercises

You won't need to understand everything that is said in a recording to answer the questions. To help you, the question paper gives you information about who is speaking, to whom, or where they are or why they are having the conversation. There will also be 15 seconds for you to read the two questions.

To help you 'tune in' to what you are going to hear you can start to make a few predictions as you read.

Here is the introductory sentence and the two questions for a Part 1 task. Read them then answer questions 1 to 6.

You'll see that you can get a good 'feel' for what you are going to hear by just thinking about the task and asking yourself a few questions.

Extract One (handbook)

You will hear a financial analyst talking on a radio programme.

1   What is going to be the focus of today's programme?

    A   measuring the performance of companies before mergers
    B   identifying the companies most likely to be involved in mergers
    C   analysing why financial institutions are encouraging mergers

2   What is the speaker's view about the prospect of more cross-border mergers?

    A   She has an open mind about how well they will work.
    B   She doubts that there will be as many as people think.
    C   She regards them as a positive development at this time.

Questions

1   Are you going to hear a monologue or a dialogue?
2   Will you hear male or female voices?
3   What is the general topic of the radio programme?
4   In the first question are you listening for a fact or an opinion?
5   In the second question are you listening for a fact or an opinion?
6   In the second question, which option, A-C, is positive, which is negative and which is neutral?

Answers

1   It's going to be a monologue (a financial analyst / the speaker)

2   It's going to be a female speaker (she)

3   Mergers

4   A fact – the focus of the programme

5   An opinion – (the speaker's view)

6   A is neutral, B is negative and C is positive

Now listen to the extract.

For each question, mark one letter (A, B or C) for the correct answer.

Listen to track 1 on CD 1

Answers to Extract One

	Comment
1B	The answer is not A - while the programme may consider performance *'cash reserves and debt'*, it is not the *'focus'* of the programme. Neither is there going to be any extensive analysis of the role of financial institutions in backing mergers (C) during the programme. The answer (B) is stated in the script – *'In today's programme, we identify Europe's top takeover targets.'*
2C	The answer is not A – when she says *'they may just well be right'* she is talking about the importance and scale of future possible mergers, not their success. Similarly, she is not questioning the number of future mergers. The speaker says, *'But one thing is for certain, Europe needs some cross-border activity. Scaling up is a necessity if Europe's big businesses are to compete with their US counterparts...'* which supports the answer C.

Now do the same for the following extract. Answer the questions before you listen to the recording.

Extract Two (handbook)

You will hear an accountant asking an IT consultant for advice about software packages.

3   Why does the consultant advise the accountant not to buy a tailored software package?

   A   The lack of training materials will cause him problems.

   B   Some parts of the product will not have been tested.

   C   Development of the software is likely to take too long.

4   According to the consultant why do producers dislike tailoring software?

   A   It may be difficult to provide adequate technical support.

   B   The profit margins are lower than on standard software.

   C   Tailored software is too expensive for most potential customers.

Questions

1   Will you hear a monologue or a dialogue?
2   Are you listening for reasons to do or not to do something?
3   Which speaker provides the answers to question 3?
4   Which speaker provides the answers to question 4?

Answers

1   A dialogue between an accountant and an IT consultant.
2   Reasons NOT to do something
3   The IT consultant
4   The IT consultant

Now listen to the extract.

For each question, mark one letter (A, B or C) for the correct answer.

Listen to track 2 on CD 1

Answers to Extract Two

	Comment
3B	While the woman does talk about the lack of training materials she points out that this won't be a problem for the accountant, who is *'computer literate'*, so the answer is not A. She also mentions the time factor but again says *'this may or may not be a problem for you.'* So the answer is not C. The answer is given in the script – *'The major drawback, though, is that while the original product goes through a series of trials…this isn't the case with the tailored elements…'* So B is the answer.
4A	The answer is A – the woman says – *'they have to consider the problems of ensuring that future upgrades work properly in your system…'* The answer is not B because she says it *'isn't so much a question of the profit margin…'* and it is not C either. The idea of increased expense is introduced by the accountant when he says *'but surely if you pay enough…'*

Now do this task.

Extract Three (May 2007 test)

Listen to track 3 on CD 1

You will hear two partners at an investment bank discussing a candidate they have just interviewed for a job.

5   Which quality does the man think is particularly valuable in the candidate?

   A   His potential for promotion to a leadership position
   B   His breadth of post-qualifying experience
   C   His willingness to work as part of a team.

6   What is the woman's reservation about the candidate?

   A   He is not experienced in an audit environment.
   B   He is not entirely confident in using their software.
   C   He is not committed to working in banking.

Answers to Extract Three

	Comment
3C	The answer is not A – the man says *'it's still fairly early to say whether he's leadership material…'* It's also not B because he says, *'he's only got the minimal amount of experience required after qualifying…'* The answer, C is supported in the recording when the man says, *'…useful member of our financial team…he demonstrated the skills needed for that kind of co-operation and he's clearly ready to take on the challenge.'*
4A	The answer is A because the woman says – *'I wonder if he's had enough involvement in an audit environment though…'* The answer is not B because she was *'impressed by his…knowledge'* of their software. Neither is it C, she says, *'he does clearly see his future in investment banking.'*

Listening Part 2

What do I have to do?

Listen to a 3-4 minute recording and answer five questions on it. There is an introductory sentence written on the question paper and given on the recording that tells you who is talking and why or about what. You'll have 45 seconds before the recording starts to read through the questions. All of the questions are multiple choice, with three options, A-C and they follow the same order as the information given in the recording. As you did in Part 1, you'll have to think about all of the options carefully before deciding on your answer. You'll hear the recording twice.

What listening texts are used?

Discussions and interviews between interacting speakers.

What is being tested?

Understanding gist, specific information, attitude, opinion, agreement and disagreement.

How many questions/marks are there?

5 questions for 5 marks – 1 mark each

How should I prepare for Part 2?

▶   Because this is one of the longer parts in the test, try to get a lot of practice listening to longer interviews and discussions, on the radio or TV.

▶   Think about how discussions move from one aspect of an issue to another as different speakers take their turn at talking, introduce different view points, agree and disagree.

▶   Practise paraphrasing the words in the questions, especially the language of expressing opinions, feelings and degrees of certainty.

Listening Part 2– Exercises

In Part 2 of the ICFE Test of Listening the conversation is quite long, 3-4 minutes. But to help you find your way through the recording, so that you know where you are, there will be cues – words and phrases in the recording that match the words and phrases in the question. These cues may be given by either speaker.

Look at the introduction and the questions from a Part 2 Listening task. First, underline the key words and phrases in the first part of each question (not options A-C) that you think will help you find your way through the conversation and help you find the right answer. Then decide which of the two speakers will give the answer.

Part 2 Exercise (handbook)

You will hear a conversation between two colleagues, Giovanni and Helga, about a seminar on Intellectual Property (IP) Rights which Helga has attended.

7   According to Helga, the best way for a company to maintain high IP value is by

    A   retaining its best staff
    B   setting up good internal systems
    C   having a flourishing research culture

8   According to the seminar speaker, an IP valuation is most often requested when

    A   people want to sell their stake in the company
    B   one company wants to take over another
    C   a company wants to float on the stock exchange

9   According to the seminar speaker, what tends to be the attitude of financiers to companies with IP assets?

    A   They charge them much higher interest rates on loans
    B   They avoid lending them large amounts of money
    C   They carry out more thorough checks before lending to them

10   Helga believes that existing trademark legislation is not helpful with IP because

    A   it hasn't been updated
    B   it is restricted to other types of company assets
    C   it is difficult to enforce

11 Helga says that the main message of the seminar was that companies should ensure that they both

    A   develop new ideas and protect established ones.

    B   protect an idea and demonstrate its marketability.

    C   protect IP assets and more tangible property.

Before you listen to the recording, here is a jumbled list of the cues that you will hear in the recording – match each cue with a question (7-11).

Cue	Question number
…but how do you measure IP value?… an IP valuation…	
…his main point… the overriding message…	
…existing trademark and copy legislation…	
…very high value…	
… finance providers will lend …	

Listen to track 4 on CD 1

Listen to track 4 on your CD and do the task.

Remember, you know that Helga will give all the answers but the cues may come from either Helga or Giovanni.

Guide to answers to Part 2 Exercise

7   According to Helga, the best way for a company to maintain high IP value is by…

    Helga will give the answer.

8   According to the seminar speaker, an IP valuation is most often requested when …

    Helga will give the answer.

9   According to the seminar speaker, what tends to be the attitude of financiers to companies with IP assets?

    Helga will give the answer.

10   Helga believes that existing trademark legislation is not helpful with IP because…

    Helga will give the answer.

11   Helga says that the main message of the seminar was that companies should ensure that they both…

    Helga will give the answer.

Cue	Question number
…but how do you measure IP value?… an IP valuation…	8
…his main point… the overriding message…	11
…existing trademark and copy legislation…	10
…very high value…	7
… finance providers will lend …	9

Answers to Part 2 –Intellectual Property

	Comment
7B	Helga says, *'But now I realise that IP really resides in systems – in clear documentation and transmission of knowledge.'* The answer is not A, Giovannni introduces the idea of staff but Helga says *'you'd think IP value would reduce. But…'* suggesting that it doesn't. The answer is not C either – the only reference to research is using *'researcher'* as and example of a valuable member of staff.
8A	Helga says, *'..acquisitions aren't really the main reason for wanting to establish IP value – not for Stock Exchange flotations either…'* therefore the answer is neither option B or C. She goes on to say IP valuation is, *'…being asked for mainly when company backers want to withdraw and realise their investment.'* So the answer is A.
9C	The answer is C as Helga says *'finance providers…tend to charge an additional amount to do a more searching audit.'* This is not a charge of higher interest rates so A is wrong. B is incorrect because she says, *'finance providers will lend whatever amount is required…'*
10C	The answer is C – *'It can involve a long and painful process through the courts as people try to make use of the legislation.'* The fact that they are using the legislation for IP makes A and B wrong.
11B	The answer is given by Helga when she says, *'it's not just a question of protection but also of showing market value…a protected idea with no proven sales value is useless.'* Making B correct and A and C wrong as they are about having new ideas and protecting them or just protecting two different types of assets.

Now try this Part 2.

Listen to track 5 on CD 1

Remember to:

▶   think about who will give the answers

▶   underline the key words and phrases that will help cue the information you need

▶   look for the answer that paraphrases the information you hear.

You will hear a conversation between two colleagues, Annette, a technician, and Tom, a senior accountant, about Parcoe Metals Inc, one of Annette's clients.

For questions 7-11, choose the best answer A, B or C.

Play the recording twice.

7   Annette is worried because Parcoe's Return on Capital Employed

   A   has fallen for the second year running.
   B   is lower than the industry average.
   C   will have a negative effect on shareholders.

8   What does Annette say about Parcoe's receivables' collection period?

   A   It reflects the fact that the company has some bad debts.
   B   It has remained unchanged for two years.
   C   It shows a need for better management of working capital.

9   What does Annette refer to in connection with Parcoe's payables payment situation?

   A   new credit control procedures
   B   improvements in payment period
   C   problems in the company's cash position

10 What does Annette suggest as a possible explanation for the change in Parcoe's operating costs?

   A   larger bills for the upkeep of its equipment
   B   the purchase of more up-to-date plant
   C   a decrease in the efficiency of machine operators

11 What is the situation regarding Parcoe's inventory management?

   A   It keeps inventory for a shorter period than is usual in the industry.
   B   It is working to reduce the quantity of goods it keeps in inventory.
   C   It intends to improve its control of inventory management.

Answers to Part 2 – Parcoe Metals Inc

	Comment
7B	A is incorrect because two years ago their results were satisfactory and the fall only happened last year. C is incorrect because Annette says, '…there's no sign of nervousness amongst the investors.' B is correct because their Return on Capital Employed is 'well below that for the sector as a whole.'
8C	A is correct because Annette says she thinks the receivables collection period is an 'important element in the assessment of the management's control of its working capital' and then says tighter controls are needed. A is wrong - Annette is just worried that bad debts could be a future possibility if nothing is done. B is wrong because we know that they changed their receivable period from 60 to 65 days.
9B	B is correct – the improvements are the reduction in payable days to bring it closer to the sector benchmark. No new procedures are mentioned and the reference to 'cash' is in connection to the company being able to reduce its reliance on creditors, so A and C are incorrect.
10A	A is correct because Annette suggests 'it may be that the company has ageing plant, and, if that's the case, maintenance charges are probably on an upward trend.' Annette is going to find out if there's been a change in efficiency but not for machine operators specifically, so C is wrong. B is wrong because no new plant has been bought.
11A	Annette gives the answer when she says Parcoe was 'holding less than one month's supply…as opposed to the industry average of 38 days.' It's inventory management is already good, so doesn't need improving, making C wrong. The company's general inventory 'looks ok', so it doesn't need to reduce the quantity it holds, making B wrong.

Listening Part 3

What do I have to do?

Listen to an informational text that is 3-4 minutes long and answer nine questions on it. There are notes written in full sentences on the question paper and you listen to the recording to find the specific pieces of information to complete the sentences. You'll have a minute before the recording starts to read through the sentences. All of the sentences follow the same order as the information given in the recording. As you listen you have to find the specific information to complete the sentences and write up to three words in the gap. You'll hear the recording twice.

What listening texts are used?

Monologues, such as speeches and presentations.

What is being tested?

Following the main points and finding specific information from the listening text.

How many questions/marks are there?

9 questions for 9 marks – 1 mark each

How should I prepare for Part 3?

▶ Practise listening to longer speeches and presentations, on the radio or TV, and making brief notes on the main points.

▶ Use the one-minute preparation time to look at all the sentences carefully and think about the kind of information that will go in the gap.

▶ Practise writing clearly, in capital letters with correct spelling, and double check as you listen for the second time whether the answer is singular or plural and is no more than three words long.

Part 3 Exercise

One of the best things you can do before you hear the recording is to try to guess what kind of word or words will go in the gap. Using your one-minute preparation time in this way will help you to both have a good idea about the topic of the talk you are going to hear but also the kind of word(s) you'll have to listen out for.

Before you listen to the Part 3 task which follows, answer these questions.

1   Looking at the introductory rubric first, what words come into your head when you think about a 'talk to shareholders about last year's performance'? Make a list of the words you think of.

2   Look at questions 12 to 16. Which are going to be positive things about the company and which are going to be negative?

3   Look at question 17 – how many different types of hotel can you think of?

4   For question 18 – what do companies need to find for their hotels?

5   For question 19 – what could be improved by making a change to a menu?

6   For question 20 – what sort of benchmark measures are used for hotels?

Discussion of possible answers for Exercise 3

1   Here are some words you may have thought of – profits / losses / share price / annual report / market share / investment / improvements / growth etc. By brainstorming different vocabulary you help to set the scene and prepare yourself for what you are going to hear.

2   12 and 13 are positive things and 14 – 16 are going to be negative things (nouns) about the company's performance over the past year.

3   Luxury / budget / city-centre / country etc. – you are going to be listening out for an adjective that describes a kind of hotel.

4   Hotels need managers / customers / staff etc

5   Number of covers (in a restaurant) / food quality – this will be a noun related to menus

6   This could be any number of things that need to be increased (bring up in the notes) such as occupancy rates / customer loyalty / staff training etc.

Listening Part 3 – Exercises

Now try this Part 3.

Listen to track 6 on CD 1

Questions 12 – 20

▶ You will hear the chairman of a hotel and entertainment group talking to shareholders about the group's performance in the last year.

▶ For questions 12 – 20, complete the sentences using up to three words.

▶ You will hear the recording twice.

ANNUAL REVIEW – ROXFORD HOTEL AND ENTERTAINMENT GROUP

Results:

12   In the Roxford Group as a whole, positive outcomes included significant increases in pre-tax profits, earnings per share and the ....

13   In the hotel division there was a continuing .... in trading.

Negative factors:

14   The Group suffered from unfavourable .... for most of the year.

15   There was a slight rise in .... in the entertainment division.

16   There were longer .... in some entertainment venues.

Changes in assets:

17   A new chain of .... hotels was set up.

UK Hotels:

Six UK hotels were sold.

18   .... were found for five hotels.

The remaining UK hotels:

Thirty five were refurbished.

19   .... was improved by making changes to menus.

20   Efforts were made to bring .... up to the industry norm.

Answers to Part 3 – Annual review – Roxford Group

Question	Answer	What the speaker said
12	(final) dividend	*I'm pleased to be able to announce a final dividend of 9.6 pence…*
13	recovery	*…the year saw operating profit rise by 17 per cent to £171 million, as the recovery in overall trading which began two years ago continued.*
14	exchange rates	*…several negative factors … for much of the year exchange rates were less favourable…*
15	operating costs	*A further negative factor was the fact that the entertainment division saw operating costs edge upwards …*
16	opening hours	*This increase was necessary because of the extended opening hours in a number of new entertainment venues …*
17	budget	*Now turning to our assets our major investment last year was in launching a new chain of hotels. Unlike our existing establishments, which are mostly four star, these are in the budget category…*
18	tenants	*Six were sold and the other five leased to tenants…*
19	catering	*Our remaining 35 hotels … We also started a rolling programme to enhance the catering in those hotels, introducing new menus…*
20	staff retention	*Measures were also taken to improve staff retention, which was low in comparison with the hotel sector as a whole.*

Don't let little mistakes lose you marks!

In Part 3 of the ICFE Test of Listening you have to write the words (up to three) you hear the speaker say. They will be the exact words you hear – you don't have to change a verb into a noun or a plural noun into a singular noun. The word(s) you hear should fit grammatically into the sentence on the question paper. But you will be expected to spell correctly, and both British and U.S. spellings will be accepted.

You must make sure that you don't make the mistake of putting the right answer but not getting the mark because the examiner can't read your writing, so it is safer to always use capital letters.

Look at this example of one candidate's answers to the Part 3 task about the Roxford Group.

How many marks out of 9 would you give this candidate? Put a tick if you think their answer is correct or a cross if you think it's wrong.

Question	Answer	Tick or cross?
12	DIVIDEND	
13	*Recovery*	
14	EXCHANGE RATE	
15	OPPERATING COSTS	
16	OPENING HOURS	
17	buget	
18	tenant	
19	catering	
20	staff	

Answers for: 'Don't let little mistakes lose you marks!'

Question	Answer	Tick or cross?	Reason for the mark
12	DIVIDEND	✓	Because 'final' is in brackets in the answer key it means that candidates do not need to write it in order to get the full mark.
13	*Recovery*	✗	This answer cannot get a mark because it is not clearly written, therefore the examiner can't read it to know whether it is correct or not.
14	EXCHANGE RATE	✗	This is incorrect because the speaker said 'rates' (plural)
15	OPPERATING COSTS	✗	The candidate has made a spelling mistake – 'operating' only has one 'p'.
16	OPENING HOURS	✓	This is correctly spelt, a correct plural (hours) and easy to read because the candidate used capital letters.
17	buget	✗	The candidate made a common spelling mistake, missing the 'd' from 'budget'.
18	tenant	✗	Although this is not in capital letters it is easy to read but the candidate should have made it plural, 'tenants'.
19	catering	✓	This is correct and easy to read.
20	staff	✗	'staff' is only part of the answer – the candidate did not write 'retention' so cannot be given the mark

Now try this Part 3.

Listen to track 7 on CD 1

Remember to:

▶ use the preparation time to think about the kind of words you need to listen for

▶ write up to three words in each gap

▶ use the second listening to check whether the answer is singular or plural and that it fits grammatically in to the gapped sentence.

Questions 12 – 20

You will hear a lecturer introducing a case study to a group of finance students.

For questions 12 – 20, complete the sentences using up to three words.

You will hear the recording twice.

CASE STUDY: COLLAPSE OF DALTON'S ELECTICAL GOODS CHAIN

Background

Dalton's had been facing greater competition from some (12) .... for several years.

Previous attempts to (13) .... Dalton's or re-finance the business had failed.

The collapse

Dalton's was unable to make (14) .... payments which were due.

Staff were afraid that the (15) .... that was run by ISQ Insurance would be short of money.

ISQ Insurance stated that the scheme was administered by a (16) .... who was external to Dalton's.

McDougall Capital

At the time of the collapse, Dalton's belonged to MacDougall Capital, a (17) .... firm.

MacDougall believed it was entitled to receive (18) .... in connection with its purchase of Dalton's.

MacDougall found a number of serious (19) '................................' in Dalton's accounts.

MacDougall claimed to have found a total (20) .... of £3.7 m.

Answers to Part 3 – Case Study – Dalton's

Question	Answer	What the speaker said
12	supermarkets	*For several years Dalton's had been suffering from increased competition from a number of supermarkets, several of which…*
13	restructure/re-structure	*Dalton's directors had made attempts to restructure the business but without success. Eleventh-hour attempts to come up with a satisfactory refinancing plan also failed.*
14	interest	*When it became clear that Dalton's was about to default on interest payments to the banking group…*
15	pension fund/ pension scheme	*Staff…were concerned that deductions from their salaries in the previous two months had yet to arrive in the pension fund operated by …ISQ Insurance.*
16	trustee	*However, ISQ Insurance gave assurances that the scheme was deposited with an external trustee, and so…*
17	private equity	*The failure of the company also prompted bitter recriminations from MacDougall Capital, the private equity business which owned Dalton's.*
18	damages	*In a legal statement it said that it intended to commence legal action to recover damages resulting from its acquisition of Dalton's…*
19	(gross) irregularities	*MacDougall claimed that inspection of the accounts for the six years prior to its purchase of Dalton's had brought to light what it referred to as 'gross irregularities'.*
20	deficiency	*…at the time MacDougall took ownership of the business, there was a deficiency of three point seven million pounds…*

Listening Part 4

What do I have to do?

Listen to five short extracts of five different speakers that are linked by theme and answer ten questions on them. There are two tasks to complete as you listen. You'll have 40 seconds before the recording starts to read through the two tasks on your question paper. As you listen you have to match the speaker with one of the six opinions, reasons, outcomes etc. listed on the question paper for each task. You'll hear the whole series of recordings twice.

What listening texts are used?

A series of five themed monologues of approximately 30 seconds each.

What is being tested?

Identifying speakers and topics, understanding context and recognising attitude, reason for speaking, gist and main points.

How many questions/marks are there?

10 questions for 10 marks – 1 mark each

How should I prepare for Part 4?

▶   Make sure you understand the meaning of a range of words used to report attitudes and feelings.

▶   Practise listening for just the general point and to get the gist of how the speaker feels or what their general opinion is; this means not worrying about knowing the meaning of every word you hear.

► Use the 40-second preparation time to think about the theme of the texts and try to guess the kinds of attitudes and opinions you are going to hear.

The Part 4 task is quite challenging because it has two elements to it.

Here are some tips for doing the task.

Do not be tempted to do task one on the first listening and task two on the second – you won't give yourself any time to check your answers. Therefore, do both tasks during the first listening then use the second listening to answer any question you missed and to check your answers.

Do not do the task by a process of elimination – just because you think C is the answer to question 21, still consider it for questions 22 to 25. If C was not in fact the answer to 21, your mistake could have a knock-on effect if you eliminate C from the beginning.

Be aware that in the recording you might hear the answer to task two before the answer to task one. Unlike the other parts in the ICFE Test of Listening, the recording does not follow the order of the questions.

Listening Part 4 – Exercises

Now try this Part 4.

Listen to track 8 on CD 1

Questions 21 – 30

You will hear five short extracts in which five different people are talking about books on accountancy.

TASK ONE – THE REASON FOR BUYING THE BOOK

For questions 21 – 25, choose from the list A – F the reason each speaker gives for buying the book.

TASK TWO – THE OUTCOME OF READING THE BOOK

For questions 26 – 30, choose from the list A – F the outcome for each speaker of reading the book.

You will hear the recording twice. While you listen you must complete both tasks.

A	to help develop a company tax strategy	Speaker 1.... (21)	A	I decided to set up my own business.	Speaker 1.... (26)
B	to help prepare documents for a takeover	Speaker 2.... (22)	B	I applied for promotion within my department.	Speaker 2.... (27)
C	to find out more about specific tax issues	Speaker 3.... (23)	C	I learned how to complete some tasks more quickly.	Speaker 3.... (28)
D	to explore implications of the disposal of assets	Speaker 4.... (24)	D	I applied for a position with another firm.	Speaker 4.... (29)
E	to prepare a risk assessment report	Speaker 5.... (25)	E	I carried out research into a particular field.	Speaker 5.... (30)
F	to explore factors affecting operational costs		F	I gained confidence in my professional ability.	

Answers to Part 4 – books on accountancy

Question	Answer	What the speaker said
21	E	*But I'd just carried out a risk analysis to do with changes in our production system, and I was having difficulty writing it up. So when I saw that the book had a section on how to write that type of report, I bought it.*
22	B	*I didn't actually buy it then, but a couple of months ago I remembered his recommendation when we were working towards the acquisition of one of our competitors*
23	C	*I'd bought it on the recommendation of a colleague, because she said it had a lot of material on tax law, which was an area I knew little about, but felt I ought to.*
24	F	*She mentioned the possible impact on running costs, and I wanted to go into that in greater detail, which was why I bought the book.*
25	D	*The previous management had bought property and companies abroad, but then there was a change of strategy, and I was in a team responsible for selling them off. I needed to learn more about the potential effects on the business of doing that, so I bought this book.*
26	C	*…and that has saved me a lot of time – even when I'm writing letters or emails.*
27	D	*I learnt a lot from it that I felt I couldn't use in my present job. So I contacted a company which seemed likely to offer me greater scope, and I was taken on.*
28	E	*Actually I got so interested in it that I started to work on a comparative study of legislation in certain member states of the European Union.*
29	F	*…much to my surprise I found that I'd already thought of most of the points myself. So I realised that I must be better at my work than I'd imagined.*
30	A	*I decided I needed a change, and started a consultancy advising other utilities, using the knowledge I'd acquired from the book.*

Words that communicate feelings

In this part of the test you may be asked to match each speaker with how they felt about something to do with their job.

Look at this group of words that describe how someone is feeling.

Put them into three groups. The first group should contain the words which suggest something negative, the second should contain words with positive connotations and the third should have words that don't fit into either of those groups.

amazed	confused	confident	worried	cautious	realistic	impressed
annoyed	excited	concerned	relieved	anxious	hopeful	delighted
nervous	proud	doubtful	frustrated	indifferent	satisfied	furious

Answers to 'Words that communicate feelings'

Group 1 - negative	Group 2 - positive	Group 3
confused / worried / cautious / annoyed / concerned / anxious / nervous / doubtful / frustrated / furious	confident / impressed / relieved / hopeful / delighted / proud / satisfied /	amazed / realistic / indifferent

For the group-3 words whether they have suggest a positive or negative feeling will often depend on context – you can be amazed by something bad as well as by something good!

Remember, with some of these words, the presence of a 'not' in front of them will give the opposite meaning: 'I wasn't confident about the outcome of the meeting.' 'He wasn't worried about finding a new manager for the department.'

Now try this Part 4.

Questions 21 – 30

You will hear five short extracts in which five different people are giving advice about investing in various companies.

TASK ONE – THE COMPANY'S PAST PERFORMANCE

For questions 21 – 25, choose from the list A – F the comment each speaker makes about the company's past performance.

TASK TWO – THE REASON FOR NOT INVESTING

For questions 26 – 30, choose from the list A – F the reason each speaker gives for not investing in the company.

You will hear the recording twice. While you listen you must complete both tasks.

A	It has maintained steady growth	Speaker 1.... (21)	**A**	Its right to use a product is disputed.	Speaker 1.... (26)
B	It has maintained market share	Speaker 2.... (22)	**B**	Its new ventures abroad may be difficult to maintain.	Speaker 2.... (27)
C	It has improved its management systems.	Speaker 3.... (23)	**C**	It operates in a declining sector.	Speaker 3.... (28)
D	It has acheived vertical integration.	Speaker 4.... (24)	**D**	It is heavily in debt.	Speaker 4.... (29)
E	It has sold a loss-making division.	Speaker 5.... (25)	**E**	Its profit margins are likely to be squeezed.	Speaker 5.... (30)
F	It has made money through exploiting its rights to patent.		**F**	Its shares are over priced.	

Answers to Part 4 – investment advice

Question	Answer	What the speaker said
21	F	...and it's made a fortune through licence agreements...
22	E	It recently found a customer for its freight business, which had been losing money for several years.
23	D	...mainly through a merger with its major supplier and another with a High-Street printing service. As a result it now sells direct to the end-user, which greatly reduces its dependence on retailers...
24	A	In the five years it's existed, Alliance Steel has done quite well: it's attracted some new customers, and its bottom line has shown healthy – while not spectacular - year-on-year increases...
25	B	...but while customers have been deserting one or two of the biggest companies in favour of some smaller players, Jaycourt had held onto its position.
26	B	...the company has set up several overseas subsidiaries, but I suspect it'll only be in a position to sustain these for a limited time...
27	F	Although its stock market performance is currently among the best in its sector, in my opinion, this is an exaggerated response to past success, and I really can't see any reason for it to continue.
28	A	...it's currently being sued by a company called Jackson. The allegation is that Markway failed to pay for permission to print with software which Jackson had patented.
29	C	Its competitors are beginning to feel the chill wind of falling demand, and it seems to me that Alliance has nothing to save it when other steel firms are already going under.
30	E	...rises in the prices of raw materials will soon feed through, and I really don't think Jaycourt is in a position to pass these on to the consumer – it will simply have to absorb them.

Speaking

Contents of the Speaking section

Introduction to Speaking

The ICFE Test of Speaking

In this section you will:

▶ Find out what you have to do in the ICFE Test of Speaking
▶ Focus on each part of the Test of Speaking by looking at examples
▶ Think about how to prepare yourself for the Test of Speaking
▶ Learn what the examiners look for in a good ICFE Test of Speaking candidate
▶ Have a go at doing a Test of Speaking

What do I have to do in the ICFE Test of Speaking?

You'll take the test with one other ICFE candidate and there'll be two examiners in the room with you as well. In this controlled but friendly environment you'll have the chance to demonstrate your language skills in a number of different contexts.

One of the examiners, called the 'interlocutor', will ask you and your partner questions and set up the tasks while the other examiner, called the 'assessor', will simply listen to what you and your partner say.

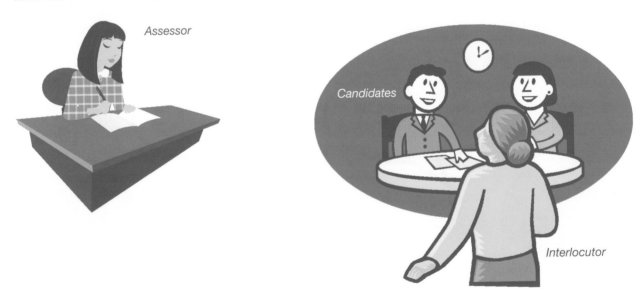

Assessor

Candidates

Interlocutor

Both of the examiners will give you marks but the interlocutor will give a global mark based on an overall impression of your speaking while the assessor will give a more detailed assessment of your performance in the test.

The test will last for 16 minutes.

Sometimes, if there's an odd number of candidates taking the test at a test centre, the last group will be a group of three candidates and two examiners.

Don't worry. The test will be the same format. However, instead of 16 minutes, the test will last for 23 minutes, so that you all get a chance to talk.

We'll look at assessment later in this section on pages 216 – 217.

The ICFE Test of Speaking is divided into four parts. Each part allows you to interact with the examiner and your partner in a different way.

Part 1

In this part the interlocutor will ask you for some information about yourself, your studies and /or work experience in finance and accounting. You'll also have to give your opinion on some finance-related topics.

Part 2

In this part you'll need to speak for one minute about a finance-related topic. The topic you talk about is from a choice of two. You'll have one minute to choose and prepare what you're going to say. Your partner will get a different choice of topic.

You'll also need to listen to what your partner says as you'll have to ask them a question about what they said when they finish talking.

Part 3

In this part the interlocutor will give you and your partner some instructions for a task that you'll do together. You'll have to negotiate and collaborate with your partner.

Part 4

In this part of the test the interlocutor will introduce some topics and issues for you and your partner to talk about together.

This part of the test is called the 'interview' and lasts 2 minutes.

This part of the test is called the 'long turn' and lasts 7 minutes.

This part of the test is called the 'collaborative task' and, with part 4, lasts 7 minutes.

This part of the test is called the 'discussion' and, with part 3, lasts 7 minutes.

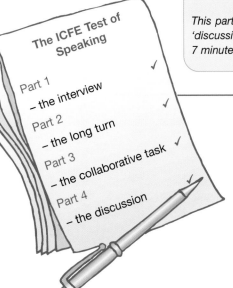

The ICFE Test of Speaking

Part 1
— the interview ✓

Part 2
— the long turn ✓

Part 3
— the collaborative task ✓

Part 4
— the discussion ✓

Speaking Part 1

In Part 1 of the ICFE Test of Speaking you should react naturally to the interlocutor's questions and try not to give answers that you have prepared before the test.

You'll need to 'think on your feet' so don't sit there in silence while you decide what to say.

Don't make your listener wait for ages to get an answer.

Often when people are asked a question they are not expecting...

> Why do you think young people are attracted to careers in your area of work?

...they 'play for time' by saying things like this.

'Well ... if you ask me... young people ...'

'That's an interesting question ... I think most young people...'

'Um... I'm not too sure, but I think that a lot of young people ...'

'Why young people are attracted to careers in my area...well I think it's because...'

Listen to track 1 on CD 2

You will hear different people 'playing for time' using the phrases above.

Exercise 1

Now you are going to use some of the 'playing for time' phrases you heard in track 1.

Listen to an examiner asking you a number of questions.

Try to respond to each of them, naturally, without stopping to think about what you're going to say.

Pause the CD after each question to give yourself time to respond.

Remember - do not just answer 'yes' or 'no' to the examiner's question. Give the reasons for your answer.

Listen to track 2 on CD 2

Speaking Part 2

In Part 2 of the ICFE Test of Speaking you'll have one minute to choose a topic to talk on and prepare what you're going to say.

Then you'll have to talk for one minute.

In our day-to-day lives we don't often talk for one minute, non stop, unless we're giving a presentation. So you'll probably need quite a lot of practice.

It's also a good idea to practise making quick notes in order to organise your thoughts and plan what you want to say.

Have a look at the choice of topics below.

These are examples of the kind of tasks you'll get in Part 2 of the ICFE Test of Speaking.

Each of the tasks has a heading and three bullet points or 'prompts'. These are there to give you some extra ideas when you're preparing the topic, just in case your mind goes blank and you can't think of anything to talk about!

You do not have to use them.

Part 2 Topics

Task A

Data security

▶   the importance of keeping data secure

▶   the different risks to data

▶   how to protect data

Task B

Report writing

▶   a company's reporting structure

▶   the importance of accuracy

▶   the presentation of a report

Exercise 2

Look at the two sets of notes made by candidates doing Task A (Data security) then answer the questions below.

Set 1

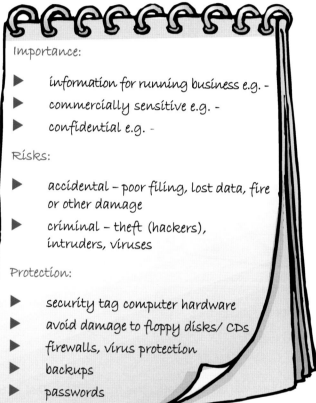

Importance:

▶ information for running business e.g. -
▶ commercially sensitive e.g. -
▶ confidential e.g. -

Risks:

▶ accidental – poor filing, lost data, fire or other damage
▶ criminal – theft (hackers), intruders, viruses

Protection:

▶ security tag computer hardware
▶ avoid damage to floppy disks/ CDs
▶ firewalls, virus protection
▶ backups
▶ passwords

Set 2

1   Data should be kept secure because it's often confidential either to the company or to individuals.

2   Data can be either lost accidentally, through poor back-up facilities or damaged hardware, or by criminals, stealing computer equipment or the stored data itself.

3   Data can be protected by using passwords and firewalls, and by having a company security policy.

Questions:

1   Which set of notes contains more points to talk about?

2   Which set of notes would be quicker to write?

3   Which set of notes is easier to read?

4   Which method of making notes do you think will be more effective for the ICFE Test of Speaking?

Answers to question 1 – 4 are on page 204.

Listen to track 3 on CD 2

Questions:

5   Which set of notes did the speaker make?

6   What did this speaker do right?

7   What could this speaker do to improve her performance?

Listen to track 4 on CD 2

Questions:

8   Did the candidate sound as though he was speaking or reading?

9   Did the candidate speak for the full minute?

10   Did the candidate cover all the points in his notes?

Answers to Exercise 2:

1. Set 1 has more points and more examples.

2. Set 1 is quicker to write – you don't have to worry about spelling or grammar – you just write the key points.

3. Set 1 is easier to read because of the layout and because it is not written in full sentences as Set 2 is. It is also easier to see how the points and ideas are organised which helps you to produce a well organised talk.

4. Set 1 will be more effective in the test situation.

5. Set 2 – she almost reads out her notes.

6. She answered the task by addressing the topic and covering the three bullet points. She used vocabulary accurately, spoke clearly and was grammatical.

7. She should speak for longer (she only spoke for 45 seconds). She could use a wider range of grammatical structures (she over used 'should be' and 'can be' in the passive). She could give more examples. She could sound more natural, more as though she was speaking, rather than reading out her notes.

8. The candidate sounded as though he was speaking.

9. Yes, the candidate spoke for the full minute. The interlocutor politely stopped him from going over time. Interlocutors will do this because they need to keep the test within the time limits, so candidates should not worry if this happens to them in the test.

10. The candidate did not cover all of the points in his notes but this is not a problem. What he did say was well structured and logically linked together.

Linking your ideas together

Your ability to use language effectively to get your ideas across is one of the skills you'll be assessed on in the ICFE Test of Speaking. The examiners will be listening to find out if you can keep on task, develop an argument and put your ideas together in a logical way.

If you can do these things the assessor will give you a good mark under discourse management, one of the four analytical criteria used by the assessor.

It's in Part 2 of the test that you'll get your best chance to show them how good you are at this.

In track 4 you heard Peter talking about data security. Here are some of the words and phrases he used to link his ideas and develop the theme of his one-minute talk:

▶ '…several reasons why…'
▶ '…also…'
▶ 'Lastly…'
▶ 'However'
▶ 'But apart from…'
▶ 'So…'
▶ 'And…'

And here are some other useful words and phrases:

▶ because	▶ therefore	▶ yet	▶ due to
▶ firstly	▶ in addition	▶ finally	▶ neither…nor
▶ as	▶ either…or	▶ in order to	▶ since
▶ though	▶ if	▶ unless	▶ although
▶ while	▶ whilst	▶ whereas	

Try to use some of them (but not too many) when you do Exercise 3.

Exercise 3

Choose either Task A or Task B and give yourself a minute to think about what you want to say.

Make some brief notes.

Task A

Performance indicators

- ▶ what performance indicators are
- ▶ how performance indicators are useful
- ▶ why managers need performance indicators

Task B

Knowing about the law

- ▶ the relationship between finance and the law
- ▶ how much legal knowledge you need
- ▶ ways of keeping up to date with legislation

Now talk for one minute on your chosen topic.

Start off by recording yourself talking. When you're more confident you could ask a friend, another student or a colleague to listen to you.

When you play back the recording of yourself, complete this feedback form by putting either a tick or a cross for each question.

Self-assessment form

1	Do I speak clearly so that every word can be heard?	
2	Do I hesitate a lot and are there long gaps where I don't say anything?	
3	Do I waste time repeating the topic and reading out the prompts?	
4	Is everything I say connected to the topic?	
5	Are there logical links between each of the points I make?	
6	Could I carry on speaking for more than a minute on this topic?	
7	Is my language informal?	
8	Is my language neutral?	
9	Is my language very formal?	
10	Do I use a range of tenses; present, past and future?	

Analysis of the self-assessment form in Exercise 3:

Your goal should be to have ticks in six of the boxes (**1**, **4**, **5**, **6**, **8** and **10**). Well done if you ticked all or most of them.

These are all skills and elements that the examiners will be hoping to hear.

1 The examiners need to be able to hear you so that they can assess you. They will be assessing your pronunciation so clear speech is important.

2 You need to keep 'on topic'. The relevance of what you say is assessed under discourse management.

5 To express an opinion or carry an argument you need to show the logical connections between the points you make. Do you want to show a *cause* and *effect*? Are you talking about a *reason* or a *purpose* or a *condition*? Your ability to do this will be assessed under discourse management.

6 Having a lot to say is generally a good thing in this part of the test and it's the interlocutor's job to stop you and to keep the test within the time limits.

8 Look at the comments on **7** and **9** below. Using mainly neutral language is the best way to approach the whole ICFE Test of Speaking.

10 This part of the test gives you the opportunity to show how comfortable you are using the English language. If you can use a range of tenses or the active and passive, for example, it will help you get a higher mark under grammar and vocabulary.

If you have ticked box **2**, remember that the examiner can only give you a mark for the language you produce; they can't assess silence! If you hesitate too much you won't get such a high mark under interactive communication. Use your one minute of planning time to get a clear idea of what you are going to say.

If you ticked box **3**, then again you are not giving yourself the full time to show the examiner what you can do. The examiner knows what's written on your task sheet so you don't have to explain it to him or her.

If you ticked boxes **7** or **9**, spend some time thinking about the impression you want to make on the examiner. If you use too much slang or informal language (which is often not precise enough to explain yourself clearly) then you may appear unprofessional to the examiner. If you use extremely formal language you will sound unnatural and possibly uncomfortable. Some words and phrases are more suitable for a written document rather than spoken language (e.g. we might write 'henceforth' but we say 'from now on').

If you want to know more about how the examiners will assess you; look at page 218

Speaking Part 3

In Part 3 of the ICFE Test of Speaking you should make sure that you and your partner don't come to a decision too quickly. Talk about each element of the task together, in some detail, before reaching a conclusion. You'll need to be able to talk together for three minutes.

Don't just agree with what your partner says or repeat the points he or she makes. It's OK to disagree or to have a different point of view.

Here's an example of the kind of task you'll get in Part 3.

PART 3

Financial Reporting

A small but fast-growing manufacturing company has asked the firm of accountants you work for to review its accounting and auditing systems. You are on the review team and you have found some major differences in the ways different sections within the manufacturing company account for and report their figures. You have been asked to address this situation.

Discussion points:

▶ the possible reasons why the different accounting and reporting methods have developed

▶ the benefits of using the same way of accounting and reporting throughout the company

▶ how to introduce changes to the way the figures are reported

---

Interacting with your partner

Being able to take your turn in a conversation, to listen to your partner and respond to what they say and to keep the conversation going if it starts to slow down or lose direction are all assessed under the heading of Interactive Communication. This is one of the four assessment criteria used by the examiners.

To find out more about assessment look at pages 216 – 219.

209

Exercise 4

Below is a list of some of the things that are assessed under interactive communication.

You will notice that the first seven in the list are things that strong candidates might do, and the last four are things that weak candidates might do.

Put a tick in the box when you hear either Peter or Helene doing any of these things during their conversation.

Listen to track 5 on CD 2 again

		Peter	Helene
1	Initiating the discussion		
2	Responding appropriately to a partner		
3	Listening to what a partner says		
4	Developing the discussion by introducing other elements		
5	Asking a partner for clarification		
6	Repairing a conversation when it begins to break down		
7	Negotiating towards a conclusion to the task		
8	Hesitating too much		
9	Dominating the conversation by speaking for too long		
10	Relying on a partner to do most of the work		
11	Simply agreeing with what a partner says		

Analysis of the form in Exercise 4

		Peter	Helene
1	Initiating the discussion		✓
2	Responding appropriately to a partner	✓	✓
3	Listening to what a partner says	✓	✓
4	Developing the discussion by introducing other elements	✓	✓
5	Asking a partner for clarification		
6	Repairing a conversation when it begins to break down		✓
7	Negotiating towards a conclusion to the task	✓	✓
8	Hesitating too much		
9	Dominating the conversation by speaking for too long		
10	Relying on a partner to do most of the work		
11	Simply agreeing with what a partner says		

1   Helene starts off by suggesting they talk about a manufacturing company in the food industry

2   Both Helene and Peter respond appropriately to each other, throughout the task. They use words and phrases like 'true' 'that's a good idea.' 'but maybe...', and they are always polite with each other.

3   They show they are listening to each other in a number of ways: by using the words and phrases mentioned in 2 above; by relating what they say to what their partner has just said and in the case of Helene and Peter, they sometimes finish off each others' sentences e.g. (Peter) ...*put things in place*... (Helene) ...*for the future*...

4   Both of them develop the conversation: e.g. Peter takes up the idea of them being food producers, then adds the idea that they have grown quickly and suggests that as a reason for them not having standardised reporting systems. Helene develops the benefits of having standard reporting systems by talking about the future benefits to the company if they go public.

5   During this conversation neither of them have to ask their partner to explain or repeat anything. However, if you don't understand a point your partner is making it's always a good idea to ask them to explain it again to you. Don't be afraid of asking for clarification during the ICFE test.

6   The conversation between Helene and Peter never really breaks down. At one point Peter seems to get a bit lost and forget what he wants to say and Helene helps to bring the discussion back to the task:

(Peter) ... *to be able to understand all the information coming to them from the different parts of the company. So ...*(pausing)

(Helene) So we need to find out from them what they need...

7   Although we don't hear the full discussion, Peter and Helene do start to negotiate over the issue of how much to change the company's reporting methods. Peter seems to be against too much change while Helene is in favour of more change if it is needed.

8   Neither of the candidates hesitates during their conversation. Any pauses they make are completely natural.

9   Neither of the candidates talks for longer than the other. They share the discussion equally.

10   Both of the candidates work equally hard at the task.

11   Both of the candidates have slightly different views and are able to discuss them rather than simply agree (or disagree) with each other.

Speaking Part 4

In Part 4 of the ICFE Test of Speaking you and your partner will talk about some issues related to finance and accounting. The interlocutor will ask some questions and you should answer as soon as possible. If your partner is talking, you should listen carefully to what they say because the interlocutor will probably ask you, 'What do you think?' or 'Do you agree?'

This is the last part of the test and often candidates are quite tired by the time they get to it.

You'll have to be careful that you don't lose concentration.

Here's an example of the kind of questions you'll be asked in Part 4. They'll always be related to the topic of the task in Part 3. This gives you an advantage as you've already been thinking about the topic during your Part 3 discussion with your partner.

Part 4

▶   What do you believe are the essential elements of good financial statements?

▶   Is it necessary to have a standardised way of financial reporting within a company? Why (not)?

▶   What benefits do you think there are in having international financial reporting standards?

▶   How realistic is it to ask the whole world to adopt a single set of standards for financial reporting? Why (not)?

When we looked at Part 1 of the test you did an exercise on 'playing for time' and 'thinking on your feet'. The same skill applies to this part of the test.

Tips on how to keep your concentration...

▶ *Change your sitting position on your chair as Part 4 starts; preferably sitting upright and slightly forward.*

▶ *Be an active listener – that means you make silent, mental links between what you hear and what you think about your partner's opinions – 'I agree with that' 'I don't think that's right'.*

▶ *When it's your turn to talk, relate the topic to your own experience, if it's relevant.*

▶ *Don't think about the time or look at the clock – it will just distract you.*

▶ *Use body language to respond to what your partner is saying – turn your body towards them, look at them as they speak and nod your head (but don't interrupt them).*

The impression you leave the examiner with in this final part of the test is as important as the initial impression they form in Part 1. So don't allow long silences while you think about what you want to say.

Remember, you are not being tested on how much you know about finance and accounting but on your ability to communicate in English.

If you don't know much about the topic, it's OK to say so.

Exercise 5

You'll hear four candidates responding to an examiner asking the Part 4 questions above.

What do you believe are the essential elements of good financial statements?

I don't have to produce many financial statements myself yet, but my teacher always told us that they should be clear and accurate and...'

Listen to track 6 on CD 2 and answer these questions

Questions:

1   Do the candidates find these questions easy?

2   Do any of the candidates hesitate?

3   Which candidates create the best impression?

Answers

1   All of the candidates find the questions difficult because they either don't have experience of them (1), haven't thought about the issues before (2 and 4) or don't have much in-depth knowledge about the topic (3).

2   Yes, they all hesitate a little and use fillers like 'er', 'um', or repeat words, 'so…so'. However, for candidates 1, 2 and 3 the fillers and hesitations are no more or longer than a native English speaker would use when thinking about what to say.

3   Candidates 1, 2 and 3 create the best impression. Candidate 4 has the same problem as candidate 2, as she hasn't thought about the topic before, but candidate 4 does not try to answer the question.

Assessment

Let's focus on how you'll be assessed during the ICFE Test of Speaking.

You are assessed on your own performance only. The examiners look at what you do in the test and do not compare you with your partner or assess you in relation to him or her.

The interlocutor is so busy managing the test that they only give a general impression mark for you and your partner. It's the assessor who gives a more detailed assessment, based on four analytical criteria:

▶ Grammar and Vocabulary

▶ Discourse Management

▶ Pronunciation

▶ Interactive Communication

These criteria are interpreted by the examiners within the context of the Cambridge Common Scale for Speaking. For ICFE this in turn relates to the Council of Europe 'Vantage' (B2) and 'Effective Operational Proficiency' (C1) levels for general language proficiency. (B2 is a lower level than C1)

Here are the 'Vantage' and 'Effective Operational Proficiency' levels as described in the Cambridge Common Scale.

LEVEL	VANTAGE	
B2	Generally effective command of the spoken language	
	▶	Able to handle communication in familiar situations
	▶	Able to organise extended discourse but occasionally produces utterances that lack coherence and some inaccuracies and inappropriate usage occur.
	▶	Maintains a flow of language, although hesitation may occur whilst searching for language resources.
	▶	Although pronunciation is easily understood, some pronunciation features from their first language may be intrusive.
	▶	Does not require major assistance or prompting by an interlocutor.

LEVEL	EFFECTIVE OPERATIONAL PROFICIENCY	
C1	Good operational command of the spoken language	
	▶	Able to handle communication in most situations.
	▶	Able to use accurate and appropriate linguistic resources to express ideas and produce discourse that is generally coherent.
	▶	Occasionally produces inaccuracies and inappropriacies.
	▶	Maintains a flow of language with only natural hesitation resulting from considerations of appropriacy of expression.
	▶	First language accent may be evident but does not affect the clarity of the message.

As we are finance and accountancy professionals rather than linguistics experts, let's put the descriptions into lay terms.

LEVEL B2 – Vantage

When this person is in a situation they know and feel comfortable in then they communicate well. They can form sentences and groups of sentences to communicate their opinions but sometimes they may use the wrong word or make a grammatical mistake. This may result in a listener being slightly confused about what they're trying to say. They can usually speak for an extended period of time but might hesitate because they can't think of the right word or expression or may have to stop to think about how to phrase what they want to say. They can pronounce individual words and groups of words so that a listener can understand them. However their first language will sometimes influence their pronunciation, making it difficult for the listener to understand what word they are saying. In a speaking test this person may ask the examiner to clarify something or repeat a question but will need no more support than that.

LEVEL C1 – Effective Operational Proficiency

This person can communicate in both familiar and unfamiliar situations. Because they make very few grammatical mistakes and have a good vocabulary they can talk about their ideas and opinions and present an argument in a way that listeners find generally easy to follow and understand. Only sometimes do they use the wrong word or use language in the wrong context. When they're speaking for any extended period of time they only hesitate in the same way that a native English speaker would when trying to find the right word or phrase something more clearly. They may have an accent but it doesn't make it difficult to understand them.

Examining Criteria

So now we know the level of English the examiners are looking for in the ICFE Test of Speaking.

Let's look at what the examiner awards the marks for, according to the four criteria.

Grammar and Vocabulary

The examiner is looking for:

▶ range – a variety of grammatical forms and vocabulary

▶ accuracy – the correct use of grammatical forms and vocabulary

▶ appropriacy – the right grammatical forms and vocabulary being used for the different tasks

Discourse Management

The examiner is looking for:

▶ coherence – the speaker's ideas are arranged in a way that makes sense

▶ extent – the speaker talks for a length of time that's appropriate to the situation

▶ relevance – the speaker says things that are related to the task and what was said previously

Pronunciation

The examiner is looking for:

▶ stress and rhythm – important words are highlighted, words are linked together and the strong and weak syllables in words are appropriate

▶ intonation – the speaker uses intonation to communicate meaning with a pitch range that is wide enough

▶ individual sounds – the separate parts of words are said clearly enough to be understood

Interactive Communication

The examiner is looking for:

▶ initiating and responding – the speaker begins discussions, introduces new ideas and reacts to his or her partner

▶ hesitation – pauses and silences are not so long that they disrupt the interaction

▶ turn-taking – speakers talk and allow others to talk in a reasonable and appropriate way

An adequate performance

A test performance good enough to pass the ICFE Test of English is one where a candidate adds his or her own ideas to the discussion and speaks for the required amount of time. The candidate may make some mistakes in his or her grammar and vocabulary and occasionally the message may be a little difficult to follow but his or her pronunciation should not cause any problems for the listener.

The examiner is not expecting a perfect performance, just the best that you are able to do.

Speaking Sample Test

Interlocutor

Good (morning/afternoon/evening). My name is …… and this is my colleague,……

And your names are?

Can I have your mark sheets, please?

Thank you.

First of all, we'd like to know a little about you.

Ask candidates the following questions in turn.

▶   Where are you both from?

▶   *(Candidate A)*, are you working or are you a student?

▶   And what about you, *(Candidate B)*?

▶   *(Candidate A)*, tell us something about your job / the course you are studying.

▶   And *(Candidate B)*, tell us about your job / the course you are studying.

Ask each candidate one further question, as appropriate.

▶   How important is it for people to know English in your area of work/study?

▶   What are the career prospects for young people in your area of work/study?

▶   Tell us why you chose this career/this course of study.

Thank you.

Task 1

Interlocutor

Now, in this part of the test I'm going to give each of you a choice of two different topics. I'd like you to choose one of the topics and give a short talk on it for about a minute.

(Candidate A), it's your turn first. Here are your topics and some ideas to help you.

*Place **Part 2** booklets, open at the task, in front of each candidate.*

You have a minute to choose your topic and prepare your talk. After you have finished your talk, your partner will ask you a brief question about it.

 Up to one minute of preparation time

All right? Now, *(Candidate A)*, which topic have you chosen?

Candidate A

States chosen topic

Interlocutor

(Candidate B), please listen carefully to *(Candidate A's)* talk, and then ask him/her a brief question about it. *(Candidate A)*, would you like to start?

Candidate A

 One minute

Interlocutor

Thank you. Now *(Candidate B)*, can you ask *(Candidate A)* a question about his/her talk?

Candidates

 Up to one minute

Interlocutor

Thank you. (Can I have the booklets please?)

Retrieve booklets. Now select a different pair of tasks for Candidate B.

Tasks for Candidate A

Funding

▶ the type of assets companies need in order to trade

▶ how businesses raise funds

▶ the advantages of long-term funding

Financial reports

▶ the purpose of external financial reports

▶ how external financial reports are used

▶ what external financial reports should contain

Interlocutor

Thank you. Now, *(Candidate B)*, it's your turn. Here are your topics and some ideas to help you.

*Place **Part 2** booklets, open at the task, in front of each candidate.*

You have a minute to choose your topic and prepare your talk. After you have finished your talk, your partner will ask you a brief question about it.

🕐   *Up to one minute of preparation time*

All right? Now, *(Candidate B)*, which topic have you chosen?

Candidate B

States chosen topic

Interlocutor

(Candidate A), please listen carefully to *(Candidate B's)* talk, and then ask him/her a brief question about it. *(Candidate B)*, would you like to start?

Candidate B

🕐   *One minute*

Interlocutor

Thank you. Now *(Candidate A)*, can you ask *(Candidate B)* a question about his/her talk?

Candidates

🕐   *Up to one minute*

Interlocutor

Thank you. (Can I have the booklets, please?) *Retrieve booklets.*

Tasks for Candidate B

Offering credit

▶   why companies offer credit

▶   the risks involved in offering credit

▶   establishing who credit should be offered to

Cash, profit and working capital

▶   the difference between cash and profit

▶   things affecting the cash position of a business

▶   why some businesses need more working capital than others

Part 3

Interlocutor

Now, in this part of the test I'd like you to talk to each other. I'm going to describe a situation to you.

*Place **Part 3** booklet, open at **Task 21** (the chosen task), in front of the candidates.*

A large company with its own internal auditing department also pays a firm of accountants to carry out an annual external audit. A major shareholder has asked why both audits are necessary. You have been asked to discuss whether the costs of the present arrangement can be justified.

There are some discussion points to help you.

You have about three (four) minutes to discuss this.

Discussion points:

▶   the need for an internal and external auditing department
▶   the link between internal and external auditing
▶   who benefits from an internal audit

Candidates

🕐   *Approximately five seconds*

Interlocutor

Please start your discussion now.

Candidates

🕐   *Approximately three minutes (four minutes for groups of three)*

Interlocutor

Thank you. (Can I have the booklet, please?)

Retrieve booklet.

Part 4

Interlocutor

Select any of the following questions, as appropriate.

▶ Is internal auditing always necessary? Why (not)?

▶ Should internal auditors work with external auditors? Why (not)?

▶ Is a favourable external audit always a sign of a company's well being? Why (not)?

▶ Do you think that external auditors should also provide other commercial services to clients? Why (not)?

Thank you. That is the end of the test.

Suggested Answers to Speaking Sample Test

It is important to realise that there is no perfect answer to a speaking test in the way that there is to most exams and tests. Candidates could give a wide variety of answers to the same question and all be judged pefectly correct. We set out here some suggestions as to how the conversation could go were you to take the Sample Speaking test, but please appreciate that these are just suggestions and by no means a definite answer.

Part 1

2 minutes (3 minutes for a group of three)

Interlocutor	Good (morning/afternoon/evening). My name is ....X.... and this is my colleague, ...Y.... . And your names are?
Suggested response	Good (morning/afternoon/evening), I am A (forename/ surname).
Interlocutor	Can I have your mark sheets, please?
Suggested response	Here is mine.
Interlocutor	Thank you. First of all, we'd like to know a little about you. Where are you both from?
Suggested response	I come from .... originally but now I live in ....
Interlocutor	Are you working or are you a student?
Suggested response	I am working full-time as a .... and studying for my ....exams in the evening at home.
Interlocutor	And what about you?
Suggested response	I study .... at college every day because I hope soon to be a .... and get a job in the field of ....
Interlocutor	Tell us something about your work.
Suggested response	From day to day I spend most of my time .... Overall I find my job is full of variety and allows me to put what I am studying into practice. It's certainly teaching me a lot about ....
Interlocutor	And tell us about the course you are studying.
Suggested response	My course is very hard work as there are many topics to cover. Probably .... is the most enjoyable aspect of the course and the one that I think will be most useful in the long run.

Interlocutor	How important is it for people to know English in your area of work?
Suggested response	Most successful ………….s can speak English so to communicate effectively with colleagues in different countries it is very useful to be fluent in the language.
Interlocutor	How important is it for people to know English in your area of study?
Suggested response	We often have lecturers who use English and many of the textbooks are in English, so I would say it was very important if not absolutely vital.
Interlocutor	What are the career prospects for young people in your area of work/study?
Suggested response	Young people in this profession find it quite difficult to find a good first job in the field, but once they are established the chances of doing well are very good.
Interlocutor	Tell us why you chose this career / this course of study.
Suggested response	I chose to become a(n) …….. because I've always been very interested in …………………… and it gives me an excellent opportunity to have a varied and interesting career.
Interlocutor	Thank you.

Part 2

7 minutes (10 minutes for groups of three)

Interlocutor	Now, in this part of the test I'm going to give each of you a choice of two different topics. I'd like you to choose one of the topics and give a short talk on it for about a minute. ....A..........., it's your turn first. Here are your topics and some ideas to help you. You have a minute to choose your topic and prepare your talk. After you have finished your talk, your partner will ask you a brief question about it.

Topics	1 Funding
	
	   ▶ the types of asset companies need in order to trade
	   ▶ how businesses raise funds
	   ▶ the advantages of long-term funding
	
	2 Offering credit
	
	   ▶ why companies offer credit
	   ▶ the risks involved in offering credit
	   ▶ establishing who credit should be offered to

Interlocutor	All right? Now, ...A....................., which topic have you chosen?
Suggested response	I've chosen to talk about Topic 1, funding / Topic 2 offering credit.
Interlocutor	............B..........., please listen carefully to ....A.............'s talk, and then ask him/her a brief question about it. ....A............, would you like to start?
Suggested points for response to Topic 1 (1 minute)	▶ Non-current assets such as plant, machinery, premises, fixtures, vehicles and computers ▶ Current assets such as inventory, receivables and cash ▶ Equity funds: approaching current shareholders and private investors, accessing the stock market and institutional investors, approaching venture capitalists and development agencies ▶ Debt funding: bank finance and bond issues on the stock market, often in the form of secured debentures/loan stock ▶ Long-term funding means security and the ability to plan ahead; it can be used to fund part of working capital as well as investment in non-current assets

Suggested points for response to Topic 2 (1 minute)	▶ Offer credit to widen pool of customers ▶ Risks – non-payment/bad debts; high interest payments for the funding of trade credit; the costs of the credit control department and collection procedures ▶ Credit should be offered following assessment of customers' financial statements, credit rating, ongoing trading experience, credit limits and trade and bank references
Interlocutor	Thank you. Now, ………B……………., can you ask ………A……… a question about his/her talk?
Suggested questions and answers for Topic 1 (1 minute)	B Why do you believe companies need non-current assets? A To use over many reporting periods in the business in order to generate profits OR B What would you say is the ideal mix of current assets? A This depends on the business – a supermarket has high levels of inventory but low receivables, a service business holds little inventory and has comparatively high receivables OR B Do you have an opinion on what is the ideal mix of equity and debt funding? A Yes - it's not a good idea for there to be too high a gearing ratio, but the ideal mix again depends on the business. OR B Given the advantages of long-term funding, why would any business make use of short-term sources of funding such as overdrafts? A Overdrafts and such like cover short-term fluctuations in funding; if long-term funding were used for this the business would be paying interest unnecessarily

Suggested questions and answers for Topic 2 (1 minute)	B	Why would you say customers are attracted to the offer of trade credit?
	A	For the customer, trade credit represents a cheap form of short-term funding for its working capital. Many customers would simply not be able to trade without it.
	OR	
	B	The risks of non-payment – how high would you say these are?
	A	It depends on the area of business, the state of the economy and also, critically, on how good the credit control system operates. Obviously bad debts are a key risk and must be minimized.
	OR	
	B	Collection procedures cover a wide variety of things. Which do you think are the most important?
	A	For most businesses it is vital to raise invoices promptly and then to focus on any customer who breaches the credit terms in any way.
	OR	
	B	How can a business assess a customer's credit rating?
	A	It can use commercially available credit rating information but it can also perform its own credit scoring based on its personal experience of each customer, which is probably a very useful means of assessment.

Interlocutor	Thank you. Can I have the booklets, please? Now, ...B............, it's your turn. Here are your topics and some ideas to help you. You have a minute to choose your topic and prepare your talk. After you have finished your talk, your partner will ask you a brief question about it.

Topics	3 Financial reports
	
	   ▶ the purpose of external financial reports
	   ▶ how external financial reports are used
	   ▶ what external financial reports should contain
	
	4 Cash, profit and working capital
	
	   ▶ the difference between cash and profit
	   ▶ things affecting the cash position of a business
	   ▶ why some businesses need more working capital than others

Interlocutor	All right? Now, ...B..................., which topic have you chosen?
Suggested response	I've chosen to talk about Topic 3, financial reports OR Topic 4, cash, profit and working capital.
Interlocutor	............A............, please listen carefully to ....B..........'s talk, and then ask him/her a brief question about it. ....B............, would you like to start?
Suggested points for response to Topic 3 (1 minute)	▶ External financial reports are designed to help a range of users to make economic decisions ▶ Investors may use them to decide whether to buy shares, retain shares or sell them ▶ Suppliers may use them to decide whether to extend credit ▶ Managers, customers and employees, as well as the government and the public at large, may also use them ▶ They should contain a statement of financial position or balance sheet, and a statement of financial performance, also known as an income statement or profit and loss account. A statement of cash flows is usually given as well.

Suggested points for response to Topic 4 (1 minute)	▶ A company's cash balance represents all the actual, realized receipts and payments of cash to date, while its profit comprises recognizable revenue less expenses whether or not these have been realized in the form of cash.
	▶ A business's cash position is affected by how far its operating activities generate cash, by its investing activities such as purchasing non-current assets, and by its financing activities such as the raising of equity capital and the payment of dividends.
	▶ A wholesale business requires a great deal of inventory in order to operate, and it also typically has a high level of receivables as its customers are retail businesses buying on credit. It therefore requires a high level of working capital.
	▶ A service business such as a firm of accountants does not require inventory as such and so has less need of working capital.
Interlocutor	Thank you. Now, ...A............., can you ask ......B......... a question about his/her talk?
Suggested questions and answers for Topic 1 (1 minute)	A What is the role of ratio analysis in how external financial reports actually help users to make economic decisions?
	B Ratio analysis is a very useful tool for a wide range of users, for instance investors interpret ratios such as return on capital employed and earnings per share to compare the performance and financial position of alternative investment opportunities.
	OR
	A Which aspect of a report do you think suppliers would focus on most?
	B Without doubt the major focus will be on the business's liquidity so suppliers would look at cash balances, and at the relationship between current assets and liabilities. In addition, a highly geared company may be a concern to suppliers.
	OR
	A What information would employees be able to extract from external financial reports?
	B As well as information on profitability, financial stability and liquidity contained in the numerical financial statements, employees can also obtain interesting information from the chairman's written statement accompanying them, about the company's past performance and future plans and prospects.

Suggested questions and answers for Topic 4 (1 minute)	A	Are changes in the relative levels of working capital items treated as cash flows from operating, investing or financing activities?
	B	They are treated as cash flows from operating activities because a key part of the business's management operations is to make sure there is a healthy balance.
	OR	
	A	When a company sells a non-current asset it usually shows that it has made either a profit or a loss on the disposal. Why is the amount of this profit or loss not usually the same as the disposal proceeds?
	B	Because to calculate profit or loss we have to deduct the carrying amount of the asset; it is only when an asset has been fully depreciated that the disposal proceeds will be the same as the profit on disposal.
	OR	
	A	How high a level of working capital would you expect a construction contract company to have, compared with an airline?
	B	Probably both companies would have a very high level of both fixed and working capital as both of these industries are well-known for being capital-intensive.
Interlocutor	Thank you. Can I have the booklets, please?	

Parts 3 and 4

Auditing

Interlocutor	Now, in this part of the test I'd like you to talk to each other. I'm going to describe a situation to you.
	A large company with its own internal auditing department also pays a firm of accountants to carry out an annual external audit. A major shareholder has asked why both audits are necessary. You have been asked to discuss whether the costs of the present arrangement can be justified.
	There are some discussion points to help you. You have about three (four) minutes to discuss this. (5 second pause). Please start your discussion now.
Discussion points	Auditing
	▶ the need for an internal auditing department
	▶ the link between internal and external auditing
	▶ who benefits from an internal audit
Sample Discussion	A In my experience most companies of any size find that having an internal audit department is a really useful way of making sure the company has the right internal controls and that they work properly.
	B Yes, you can't really just leave it up to the external auditors as they are only around for part of the year and the scope of their audit can't be as detailed as internal audit's.
	A But sometimes they do end up duplicating each other's work so it would look like the costs are duplicated and there is therefore some wastage.
	B If this happens though it can be possible for the external auditors to satisfy themselves that the internal audit work is good enough for it to be relied upon when forming an opinion. This cuts down the external audit work.
	A I don't think it happens that much in practice to be honest, but I suppose it depends on the size and nature of the business and the strategy towards internal audit that the board has taken.
	B Also, internal audit often get involved in issues that aren't of concern to the external auditor, like planning new internal controls for a new venture.
	A That's true, and they get much more involved too in the internal business processes that don't result directly in the sort of financial statements that external auditors look at.

Sample Discussion	B	We shouldn't forget their role in risk management – in some industries it's absolutely vital that internal audit monitor the effectiveness of the risk management processes.
	A	So we agree that costs spent on internal audit are worth it, but perhaps what the major shareholder is trying to say is that the costs of the external audit are not!
	B	True, but I don't suppose the company has much option about having an external audit, it's almost certainly a regulatory requirement.
	A	Yes, and having an expert external opinion does give outsiders comfort that the financial statements present a true and fair view, which they can't really be sure of if there's no external audit.
	B	That's often said about external audit but you have to remember the expectations gap – a lot of outsiders actually think the audit opinion is a guarantee there has been no fraud or irregularity, and of course we know that's not true.
	A	If the company has good governance then the board's audit committee can work with both internal and external audit to reassure shareholders about fraud and irregularity…
	B	That's the ideal, yes…
Interlocutor		Thank you. Can I have the booklets, please?

Part 4

Interlocutor	Is internal auditing always necessary?
Suggested response (A)	No I don't believe it's always necessary.
Interlocutor	Why not?
Suggested response (A)	Because some businesses are really small and are well enough controlled by the finance department on its own.
Interlocutor	What do you think?
Suggested response (B)	I think internal audit is always necessary in some sectors, such as financial services for instance.
Interlocutor	Why?
Suggested response (B)	We mentioned risk management earlier on – it's a regulatory requirement in some cases that the business has a risk-based approach to internal controls, and internal audit plays a vital role in that.
Interlocutor	Should internal auditors work with external auditors?
Suggested response (B)	On the whole I think they should aim to co-operate, yes.
Interlocutor	Why?
Suggested response (B)	Mainly because when the external auditor can place reliance on the work of internal audit the work done by the former is less, and the quality of the audit opinion is better.
Interlocutor	Do you agree?
Suggested response (A)	Not really. However hard they try, internal audit are never truly independent of the business, so if external auditors rely on their work the independence of the external audit opinion is compromised.
Interlocutor	Is a favourable external audit always a sign of a company's well-being?
Suggested response (A)	Definitely not.
Interlocutor	Why not?
Suggested response (A)	Well, I think recent experience shows us that it's perfectly possible for a business to receive a clean audit opinion yet for it to have suffered real operational problems or even fraud, which see it go under quite a short while later.

Interlocutor	How about you?
Suggested response (B)	Sadly I think that's true, but I would say these are pretty rare occurrences – though well-publicised – and for the vast majority of companies a clean audit report is pretty reliable.
Interlocutor	Do you think that external auditors should also provide other commercial services to clients?
Suggested response (B)	I don't have a problem with this, provided the audit firm is big enough and professional enough, and it has concluded fairly on whether there is conflict of interest.
Interlocutor	What do you think?
Suggested response (A)	Realistically it's in providing other commercial services that the costs of the external audit are fully recovered – so the conflict of interest issue means it's not ideal, but we probably have to live with it.
Interlocutor	Thank you. That is the end of the test.

Reading Mock Test

TIME 1 hour 15 minutes

INSTRUCTIONS TO CANDIDATES

Do not open the question paper until you are told to do so.

There are 54 questions in this paper.

Read the instructions carefully.

Answer all questions.

Write your answers on the separate Answer Sheet at the end of the test. Use a soft pencil.

You may write on the question paper, but you must transfer your answers to the separate Answer Sheet within the time limit.

At the end of the examination, hand in both the question paper and the Answer Sheet.

INFORMATION FOR CANDIDATES

Questions 1 – 36 carry one mark each.
Questions 37 – 54 carry two marks each.

Questions 1 – 6

▶ Read the following extract about the appointment of an auditor in Poland from a book about corporate governance.

▶ Choose the best word to fill each gap from A, B, C or D below.

▶ For each question 1 – 6, mark one letter (A, B, C or D) on your Answer Sheet.

There is an example at the beginning (0).

EXTRACT: GDANSK CODE

The seventh principle of corporate governance outlined in what is (0) .... as the 'Gdansk Code' (1) .... the process by which a company's auditor is appointed in Poland. The auditor is appointed by the supervisory board and a minimum of two independent board members should support the appointment resolution. The board may appoint an audit committee, (2) .... mainly of independent board members, to monitor the company's financial situation and its accounting system.

In the code, there are some interesting provisions, which are designed to help ensure auditor independence. These (3) .... appointing a new auditor every five years, and publishing the financial (4) .... of services provided by the auditor, or its subsidiaries and affiliates, in the accounting year. It should be noted that, (5) .... appointing a new audit firm, the company may continue to use the same firm with a change of personnel to (6) .... a completely different audit team.

Example:

0	**A** known	**B** called	**C** named	**D** referred

Answer:

0	**A** [-]	**B** [ ]	**C** [ ]	**D** [ ]

Options:

1	**A** respects	**B** applies	**C** relates	**D** concerns
2	**A** composed	**B** built	**C** combined	**D** made
3	**A** contain	**B** include	**C** consist	**D** enclose
4	**A** worth	**B** profit	**C** value	**D** rate
5	**A** just as	**B** except for	**C** rather than	**D** even so
6	**A** create	**B** reach	**C** cause	**D** bring

(May 2007 paper)

Questions 7 – 12

▶ Read the following newspaper article about a British travel company.

▶ Choose the best word to fill each gap from A, B, C or D below.

▶ For each question 7 – 12, mark one letter (A, B, C or D) on your Answer Sheet.

TRAVEL FIRM'S DEBT COSTS RISE

In recent weeks there has been considerable speculation in the financial press about Sky International Travel, the troubled British package-tour operator. The company has now admitted that its debt costs are set to (7) .... by a figure in the region of £10 million a year. This (8) .... a change in the terms of its bonding and letter of credit facilities, which govern £550 million of debt. The terms (9) .... that once the company's market capitalization reaches £439 million or more for thirty (10) .... days, which it did on Tuesday of this week, Sky International Travel is (11) .... to pay fees for the facilities at rates of 2 per cent for drawn and 1 per cent for undrawn facilities. The company has also restated its financial results for the last financial year to (12) .... new accounting standards.

7	**A** extend	**B** increase	**C** develop	**D** advance
8	**A** arises	**B** results	**C** relates	**D** follows
9	**A** declare	**B** report	**C** express	**D** state
10	**A** consecutive	**B** succeeding	**C** progressive	**D** sequential
11	**A** accountable	**B** responsible	**C** liable	**D** answerable
12	**A** comply	**B** reflect	**C** regard	**D** abide

(May 2007 paper)

Questions 13 – 24

▶ Read the following extract from a chief executive's statement in a company's annual report.

▶ Identify the best word to fill each gap.

▶ For each question 13 – 24, write ONE word in CAPITAL LETTERS on your Answer Sheet. Answers of more than one word will be marked wrong, even if they include the correct answer.

There is an example task at the beginning (0).

EXTRACT: CHAIRMAN'S STATEMENT

The UK economy is fuelled (0) .... the service sector, but faces growing overseas competition from highly-qualified, lower cost talent. As a result, demand (13) .... enhanced business skills in the UK continues to grow, underpinned by an ever-increasing demand from employers for increased skills from their employees. While the number of university students in the UK (14) .... rising, employers are unable to meet their recruitment targets with appropriately qualified graduates and hence the focus on high quality business-related qualifications at the graduate and postgraduate level is increasing.

This company is well-positioned to take advantage (15) .... these trends. We already have a strong position and leading brand for providing education and training to professionals throughout their careers and for supporting organizations and professional bodies by developing (16) .... employees and members. We already work with (17) .... 90 of the top 100, companies in the FTSE 100 and most of the major accounting and law firms. We have a deep understanding of and insight (18) .... their needs and demands.

This position offers (19) .... numerous potential areas for further growth. There are opportunities for us to build further on our already strong examinations businesses both within the UK (20) .... overseas. There are opportunities for us to continue the growth of our professional development businesses, (21) .... by increasing our presence in the sectors in which we currently operate, and potentially via expanding into new areas.

There are internal opportunities for improvement (22) .... well. We will be investing in systems and associated revised processes in 2008 and anticipate benefits from this investment to flow (23) .... the middle of 2009. We will also be tightening our control on areas of major expenditure, (24) .... as property and procured goods.

Example answer:

0	B	Y																			

Questions 25 – 30

▶ Read the following extract from a report about Financial Shared Services Centres.

▶ Use the words in the box below the text to form ONE word that fits in the same numbered gap in the text.

▶ For each question 25 – 30, clearly write ONE word in CAPITAL LETTERS on your Answer Sheet.

There is an example at the beginning (0).

Example:

0	M	E	R	G	E	R	S												

EXTRACT: FINANCIAL SHARED SERVICES CENTRES

The market in which multinational companies operate is characterized by globalization, (0) ……..... , acquisitions and consolidation. All of these factors require companies to standardize operations so as to stay (25) ……..... . One way of keeping costs down and improving (26) ……..... is by moving financial functions to one (27) ……..... location: a Financial Shared Services Centre (FSSC).

When companies extended their presence across national borders, it became (28) ……..... uneconomical to maintain a duplicate accounting infrastructure within each country of operation. Decentralised companies, therefore, began to combine processes such as payroll and purchasing in one FSSC, and to sell back those services at cost to individual business units.

One problem that FSSCs have faced is keeping staff motivated, as the work tends to be repetitive. Nevertheless, the indications are that FSSCs have become a firmly established part of most businesses and this is (29) ……..... to change in the forseeable future. Companies which have set up FSSCs report a (30) ……..... in staff costs in the order of 35%.

0	MERGE	25	COMPETE	26	EFFICIENT	27	CENTRE
28	INCREASE	29	LIKELY	30	REDUCE		

(May 2007 Paper)

Questions 31 – 36

▶   Read the following notification of a company's Annual General Meeting of shareholders.

▶   Use the words in the box below the text to form ONE word that fits in the same numbered gap in the text.

▶   For each question 31 – 36, write ONE word in CAPITAL LETTERS on your Answer Sheet.

EXTRACT: NOTICE OF ANNUAL GENERAL MEETING OF SHAREHOLDERS

The Annual General Meeting of shareholders will be held on 25 January at the company's registered office for the following purposes:

▶   To approve the annual report comprising the audited accounts of the company for the financial year ended 30 September and to approve the auditor's report thereon.

▶   To approve the balance sheet and profit and loss account as of 30 September and the (31) .... of net profits.

▶   To elect persons as directors, each to hold office until the next Annual General Meeting of shareholders and until his or her (32) .... is duly elected.

▶   To elect an auditor for the ensuing year.

▶   To deal with any other business which may (33) .... be brought before the meeting.

Only shareholders on record at the close of business on 23 January are (34) .... to vote at the Annual General Meeting of shareholders and at any adjournment thereof.

Shareholders are advised that the (35) .... are not subject to specific quorum or majority (36) ....

31	ALLOCATE	32	SUCCESS	33	PROPER
34	TITLE	35	RESOLVE	36	REQUIRE

(May 2007 paper)

Part 4

Questions 37 – 42

▶ Read the statements below and the extract from an article in a newspaper discussing labour mobility.

▶ Identify which section of the extract (A, B, C or D) is referred to by each statement 37 – 42.

▶ For each question 37 – 42, mark ONE letter (A, B, C or D) on your Answer Sheet. You will need to use some of these letters more than once.

There is an example statement at the beginning (0).

Example:

0   Shortages of workers can cause delays.

Answer:

0   **A** [ ]   **B** [-]   **C** [ ]   **D** [ ]

Statements

37   More older people in their home country means people look for work overseas.

38   Both companies and workers move around internationally.

39   Companies which relocate to lower their costs can find that wage rates rise.

40   After working abroad many people go back to their original countries.

41   Workers who travel to get jobs are usually highly qualified.

42   There is labour mobility inside countries as well across borders.

EXTRACT: WORKERS OF THE WORLD ON THE MOVE

A   Globalization means that not only are companies moving operations offshore to where there is cheaper labour, but also workers are increasingly prepared to cross borders to find where the best jobs are. Popular images of migrant workers are of the poor, the oppressed and unskilled. Yet according to Manpower, one of the world's largest recruitment companies, they are more likely to be young, under 30 years of age, well-educated with university or vocational qualifications, and female as much as male. This matters to employers who, according to Manpower, will increasingly be competing for workers, such as the managers at Irish meat processing plants 'whose skilled Slovak butchers are being lured away by competitors in Norway'.

B   Unlike earlier migrations, today's migrant workers are not on a one-way trip. Flights home are readily available. Irish emigrants began returning a decade ago as the economy of the 'Celtic Tiger' boomed. Now, it is Indian professionals and Polish construction workers who are returning to seek new opportunities. Competition for such workers is increasing. Even oil-rich Gulf states can no longer rely on a seemingly endless flow of cheap engineers and construction workers from the Asian sub-continent. One Gulf company, for example, told Manpower it was 'starting to miss crucial project deadlines' because it could not 'import the skilled expatriate engineers and project managers it used to be able to get easily.'

C   Propelling labour mobility over the next few decades will be huge demographic changes, in particular the ageing and stagnating populations in developed countries. According to the United Nations, Italy's population is expected to decline from 57m to 41m by 2050 while Japan's is projected to fall 17 per cent to 105m by 2080. Workers are also becoming more aware of their worth, with the internet providing much greater information on job opportunities at home and abroad, says Manpower. Workers will also move within national boundaries to find work. China is currently struggling to accommodate 'the rush of individuals leaving its poor western provinces in search of better jobs in the glittering commercial hubs of the country's east coast,' it says. Japan has also seen a huge population shift to its cities, imperiling its agricultural sector, while 'Norway must deal with the emptying of its rural north and Mexico's southern states contend with…a massive talent drain to the industrialized northern border states.'

D   Employers who have moved offshore in search of cheap labour can get caught out, however, as local economies develop and other multinationals move in, competing for a limited number of skilled workers. According to Manpower, it is not unusual for workers at call centres in Bangladesh to attend an interview, accept a new job and start straight away at a higher salary, all in the same lunch hour. The recruitment group warns that government policies restricting inflows of migrant workers, in response to populist demands, could prove counter-productive by leaving businesses short of both skilled and unskilled labour. National immigration policies have concentrated on raising barriers to the unskilled while trying to encourage highly skilled professionals, engineers, scientists and entrepreneurs. But Manpower points out that blue collar workers are also in short supply.

By Andrew Taylor, Employment Correspondent, Financial Times Published: June 24 2008 04:51

Questions 43-48

▶ Read the following extract from an article about practice management, and the sentences following the extract.

▶ Choose the best sentence to fill each of the gaps in the extract.

▶ For each gap 43 – 48, mark ONE letter (A – H) on your Answer Sheet. Do not use any letter more than once. There are two extra sentences which you do not need to use. Sentence H is always used as the example at the beginning (0).

EXTRACT: UITF 40 – THE SPELLING OF FEAR

It may seem like yet another piece of legislation to add to the pile and another process to learn, but rather than fight compliance, accountancy firms should embrace the opportunities UITF 40 presents to improve their practice management. (0) .... Focusing on maximizing chargeable time is all very well, but it is not effective unless you have the procedures and processes in place to ensure timely billing and collection of cash.

UITF 40 is a particularly pertinent issue for accountancy firms. Previously un-invoiced or uncompleted work was described as 'work in progress' (WIP) and was based on cost value, with tax only charged once an invoice was raised. (43) .... The Consultative Committee of Accountancy Bodies (CCAB) estimates that around 25% of accountancy firms will face a tax bill that is more than 50% higher than average when they adopt UITF 40.

But before you gasp and visualize your profits running to the tax man, appreciate that implementing UITF 40 will encourage you to bank your money faster. (44) .... To avoid suffering an increased tax burden, the approach is to reduce the WIP/debtor period as much as possible.

Another tip is to monitor time levels carefully. One fundamental issue which needs changing is the fact practices often bill per hour and not for the job. Instead practices should provide a quote up-front for the entire cost of the job and manage time accordingly. That way, you have a better handle on your accounts and you manage your clients' expectations effectively. (45) .... If you neglect your timesheets and do not realise when you are over-servicing clients, you will invariably end up paying for it, either in terms of refunding a percentage of the job or by creating a disgruntled client who will take their business elsewhere.

Where timesheets are concerned, you need proactively to implement a value limit - for example, set a rule that the WIP will not go above 100 hours and set up a system which will alert you if too many hours are being charged to an account. (46) .... It sounds so obvious, but often people become so focused on timesheets they lose track of who is paying for what.

Keeping track of your invoices and tabs on your timesheets will certainly help improve your practice management and make UITF 40 less painful. Another key element to consider which transcends administration is the business of customer relationship management. How transparent is your practice? (47) .... Again, this is where you need to view your practice as a business. You cannot afford to bombard your client with jargon and abbreviations. You need to make it clear to them exactly what you are billing them for and there will be no cause for argument at the end of the contract.

A happy customer is a repeat customer. It is time we had a mini-revolution in the accountancy world. We need to operate practices as businesses, become more transparent and invest more time in customer management. (48) .... Regulation tends to pivot around issues of transparency and accountability. Get the processes in place which enable you to have easy viability of your audit trails and operate effective customer and practice management, and new legislation should be easy to adapt to.

Simon Crompton 12 Jan 2006, ACCA Accounting and Business magazine

Sentences:

A	If you agree on the price beforehand, this will avoid the client complaining that you have overcharged them and requesting a refund.
B	There are clients out there that do not have a clue what the accountant is billing them for.
C	Accountants are reluctant to bill until the job is done - this attitude needs to change.
D	Having a higher percentage or professionally qualified staff will help here.
E	UITF 40 will result in WIP valued at anticipated selling price, a 'fair value' which will increase tax liability.
F	In addition to this, it is essential to keep track of your invoices.
G	If we adopt this philosophy, it makes compliance in all areas of accountancy a lot easier to implement.
H	Accountants need to run their practices as businesses.

Example:

    0   **A** [ ]   **B** [ ]   **C** [ ]   **D** [ ]   **E** [ ]   **F** [ ]   **G** [ ]   **H** [-]

▶ Read the following extract from a text on transfer pricing, and the questions following the extract.

▶ Identify the best option as the answer to each question on the basis of what you have read in the extract.

▶ For each question 49 – 54, mark ONE letter (A, B, C or D) on your Answer Sheet.

EXTRACT: MARKET-BASED TRANSFER PRICES

In most circumstances, where a perfectly competitive market for an intermediate product exists it is optimal for both decision-making and performance evaluation purposes to set transfer prices at competitive market prices. A perfectly competitive market exists where the product is homogeneous and no individual buyer or seller can affect the market prices.

When transfers are recorded at market prices divisional performance is more likely to represent the real economic contribution of the division to total company profits. If the supplying division did not exist, the intermediate product would have to be purchased on the outside market at the current market price. Alternatively, if the receiving division did not exist, the intermediate product would have to be sold on the outside market at the current market price. Divisional profits are therefore likely to be similar to the profits that would be calculated if the divisions were separate organizations. Consequently, divisional profitability can be compared directly with the profitability of similar companies operating in the same type of business.

In a perfectly competitive market the supplying division would supply as much as the receiving division requires at the current market price, as long as the incremental cost is lower than the market price. If this supply is insufficient to meet the receiving division's demand, it must obtain additional supplies by purchasing them from an outside supplier at the current market price. Alternatively, if the supplying division produces more of the intermediate product than the receiving division requires, the excess can be sold on the outside market at the current market price.

If the supplying division cannot make a profit in the long run at the current outside market price then the company will be better off not to produce the product internally but to obtain its supply from the external market. Similarly, if the receiving division cannot make a long-run profit when transfers are made at the current market price, it should cease processing this product, and the supplying division should be allowed to sell all its output to the external market. Where there is a competitive market for the intermediate product, the market price can be used to allow the decisions of the supplying and receiving divisions to be made independently of each other.

In practice, it is likely that total company profits will be different when the intermediate product is acquired internally or externally. The supplying division will incur selling expenses when selling the intermediate product on the external market, but such expenses will not be incurred in inter-divisional transfers. If the transfer price is set at the current market price, the receiving division will be indifferent as to whether the intermediate product is obtained internally or externally. However, if the receiving division purchases the intermediate product externally, the company will be worse off to the extent of the selling expenses incurred by the supplying division in disposing of its output on the external market. In practice, many companies modify the market price rule for pricing inter-divisional transfers and deduct a margin to take account of the savings in selling and collection expenses.

One of the major problems with using market prices is that the market is unlikely to be perfectly competitive. In addition, the transferred product may have special characteristics that differentiate it from the other varieties of the same product. The market price for the intermediate product is appropriate only when quality, delivery, discounts and back-up services are identical. Furthermore, it may be possible to purchase the intermediate product in the external market from suppliers who are selling at a temporary distress price that is below total cost but above variable cost. If the supplying division has excess capacity incorrect decisions may arise because of strict adherence to the market price rule.

By Colin Drury, from Management Accounting for Business Decisions. Second edition 2003, Thomson Learning

Questions:

49   Where it is operating in a perfectly competitive market a transfer price should be set which

   A   allows decisions to be made easily

   B   is the price in the market which is most competitive

   C   evaluates performance effectively

   D   affects the market price

50   Where an organization has a division that supplies items to another division, setting the transfer price at market price will

   A   force the receiving division to buy on the outside market

   B   increase each division's profits

   C   make each division's profits comparable with those of like companies

   D   force the supplying division to sell on the outside market

51   If the supplying division cannot meet all of the receiving division's demand for the product when the transfer price is the current market price, what will happen?

A   The supplying division will incur additional costs

B   The market price will rise

C   The receiving division will incur lower costs

D   The receiving division will buy the remaining products from an external supplier

52   A receiving division which cannot operate profitably long-term when the transfer price is the market price should

A   withdraw from the market for that product

B   increase the transfer price

C   sell only to external buyers

D   be dependent on the supplying division

53   If a company purchases externally rather than internally at the current market price, its profits will decrease because

A   staff will be less motivated

B   it will cost money to make external sales

C   it will cost money to make external purchases

D   it will have to dispose of its supplying division

54   According to the final paragraph, the market price should only be used as a transfer price when

A   the market is not perfectly competitive

B   the internally-produced product is not the same as that available externally

C   the product is available cheaper externally

D   all factors involved are the same

Answer Sheet

Indicate your answers here:

1	A [ ]	B [ ]	C [ ]	D [ ]
2	A [ ]	B [ ]	C [ ]	D [ ]
3	A [ ]	B [ ]	C [ ]	D [ ]
4	A [ ]	B [ ]	C [ ]	D [ ]
5	A [ ]	B [ ]	C [ ]	D [ ]
6	A [ ]	B [ ]	C [ ]	D [ ]
7	A [ ]	B [ ]	C [ ]	D [ ]
8	A [ ]	B [ ]	C [ ]	D [ ]
9	A [ ]	B [ ]	C [ ]	D [ ]
10	A [ ]	B [ ]	C [ ]	D [ ]
11	A [ ]	B [ ]	C [ ]	D [ ]
12	A [ ]	B [ ]	C [ ]	D [ ]

Indicate your answers here in CAPITAL LETTERS:

13																	
14																	
15																	
16																	
17																	
18																	
19																	
20																	
21																	
22																	
23																	
24																	

Indicate your answers here in **CAPITAL LETTERS:**

25																
26																
27																
28																
29																
30																

31																
32																
33																
34																
35																
36																

Indicate your answers here:

37	**A** [ ]	**B** [ ]	**C** [ ]	**D** [ ]
38	**A** [ ]	**B** [ ]	**C** [ ]	**D** [ ]
39	**A** [ ]	**B** [ ]	**C** [ ]	**D** [ ]
40	**A** [ ]	**B** [ ]	**C** [ ]	**D** [ ]
41	**A** [ ]	**B** [ ]	**C** [ ]	**D** [ ]
42	**A** [ ]	**B** [ ]	**C** [ ]	**D** [ ]

43	A [ ]	B [ ]	C [ ]	D [ ]	E [ ]	F [ ]	G [ ]	H [ ]
44	A [ ]	B [ ]	C [ ]	D [ ]	E [ ]	F [ ]	G [ ]	H [ ]
45	A [ ]	B [ ]	C [ ]	D [ ]	E [ ]	F [ ]	G [ ]	H [ ]
46	A [ ]	B [ ]	C [ ]	D [ ]	E [ ]	F [ ]	G [ ]	H [ ]
47	A [ ]	B [ ]	C [ ]	D [ ]	E [ ]	F [ ]	G [ ]	H [ ]
48	A [ ]	B [ ]	C [ ]	D [ ]	E [ ]	F [ ]	G [ ]	H [ ]

49	A [ ]	B [ ]	C [ ]	D [ ]
50	A [ ]	B [ ]	C [ ]	D [ ]
51	A [ ]	B [ ]	C [ ]	D [ ]
52	A [ ]	B [ ]	C [ ]	D [ ]
53	A [ ]	B [ ]	C [ ]	D [ ]
54	A [ ]	B [ ]	C [ ]	D [ ]

Writing Mock Test

TIME 1 hour 15 minutes

INSTRUCTIONS TO CANDIDATES

Do not open the question paper until you are told to do so.

Read the instructions carefully.

Answer the Part 1 question and the Part 2 question.

Write your answers in the spaces provided on the question paper.

Write clearly in pen, not pencil. You may make alterations, but make sure your work is easy to read.

INFORMATION FOR CANDIDATES

Part 1 carries 40% of the total marks available and Part 2 carries 60% of the total marks available.

Part 1 – Question 1

You must answer this question.

You work for a firm of accountants. One of your clients, CMD plc, has a 12 month reporting period ending in two months time, on 30 September 20X3. As the firm to which CMD plc outsources its nominal ledger and payroll functions you have received the following letter from CMD plc's statutory auditor.

Read the letter from Phoebe Collinson, the partner at the firm of auditors, on which you have already made some notes. Then, using all the information in your notes, write to the auditor on behalf of your client, CMD plc.

We are planning the work to be done on the statutory audit of our mutual client, CMD plc, in respect of its 12 month reporting period ended 30 September 20X3. We require some information from you on some points.

We have audit procedures established which are based on the accounting software package you were using during the reporting period ending 30 September 20X2. We assume you have not changed this software. **← Upgraded package**

We understand from the client that they have made some major acquisitions of plant and equipment in the reporting period. Could you outline the principles that you have applied in the nominal ledger in respect of these? **← Describe**

Our client has mentioned that they used external finance to make these acquisitions and have referred us to you for more details. We need to understand the nature of this funding. **← Explain**

We understand your firm advised our client to make use of a revised set of performance indicators each month based on the balanced scorecard approach. We are not sure this approach is beneficial for CMD plc. **← Disagree - give reason**

Finally we anticipate that two members of our audit team will need to visit your premises for the second week of November 20X3. **← Confirm**

We look forward to hearing from you.

Yours sincerely

Phoebe Collinson

Partner

Write a letter of between 120 and 180 words in an appropriate style on the opposite page. Do not write any postal addresses.

Question 1

....
....
....
....
....
....
....
....
....
....
....
....
....
....
....
....
....
....
....
....
....
....
....
....
....

You must answer this question.

You work for an accountancy firm and one of your clients is an engineering company engaged in making items to order for a limited range of business clients. In the last two months the firm has experienced bad debts as its two largest clients have ceased business. Its cash flow has been severely affected. The company has asked your firm for advice concerning credit policy and cash management and you have considered its current financial position in preparing your response.

Write a **report** for the engineering company. Your report should:

▶ Describe the features of an effective credit policy

▶ Explain the effects of the bad debts on the company's cash balance and business

▶ Outline the risks the company now faces

▶ Prioritize the steps that the company should take next.

Write your answer in **200 – 250** words in an appropriate style on the following pages.

Question 2

Listening Mock Test

This entire test is presented on CD 2 as Track 7

TIME   Approximately 40 minutes

INSTRUCTIONS TO CANDIDATES

Do not open this paper until you are told to do so.

There are thirty questions on this paper.

Read the instructions carefully.

Answer all the questions.

You will have 5 minutes to transfer your answers onto the answer sheet at the end of the this test.

INFORMATION FOR CANDIDATES

This paper requires you to listen to a selection of recorded material and answer accompanying questions (on CD 2).

There are four parts to the test.

Each part of the test will be heard twice.

There will be a pause before each part to allow you to look through the questions, and other pauses to let you think about your answers.

Each question carries one mark.

Part 1

Questions 1-6

▶ You will hear three different extracts.

▶ For questions 1-6, mark one letter (A, B or C) for the correct answer.

▶ There are two questions for each extract. You will hear each extract twice.

Extract One

You will hear two colleagues discussing an insolvency case.

1   What was the man's assessment of the Talbot case before he went on leave?

    A   that it was so simple that a junior colleague could complete it

    B   that the company were trying to rush through the liquidation process

    C   that there was very little paperwork pending from the company

2   The colleagues agree that they should

    A   contact Talbot for an explanation

    B   pay the supplier the balance in full

    C   investigate the validity of the claim

Extract Two

You will hear part of a radio programme discussing risk management and insurance for the aviation industry.

3   Why does the man make a comparison between aviation insurance and home insurance?

    A   to illustrate that getting insurance for his company is an easy process

    B   to imply that his company is as responsible as any home owner

    C   to explain that his company has obligations to its financial backers

4   What does the man say about his insurance provider?

    A   He believes they charge him a reasonable rate for his insurance

    B   He is confident that they would cover any category of risk

    C   He is pleased with the advice they give him on which risks to cover

Extract Three

You will hear part of a talk by a private equity investor about different aspects of his work.

5   What is the man doing when he talks about the meetings and discussions he is involved in?

     A   Illustrating the type of private equity investment his board looks for

     B   Describing a typical working day as a private equity investor

     C   Explaining why some of his target companies need a lot of guidance

6   What point does the man make about purchasing a company?

     A   The financial records are only one of many factors when deciding to buy a company.

     B   It is often difficult to get the support of staff within the company he wants to buy.

     C   He is mainly interested in buying companies in the retail and food production sectors.

Part 2

Questions 7 – 11

You will hear a conversation between two colleagues at a firm of accountants, Katrin and Angelo, about a research report on human resource accounting.

For questions 7-11, choose the best answer A, B or C.

You will hear the recording twice.

7   Katrin thinks measuring human resource is important because

      A   it should be treated in the same way as other business resources

      B   a company's employees are its most valuable asset

      C   it helps with an organisation's strategic planning

8   Angelo says that the human resource accounting exercise he was involved with

      A   was left incomplete

      B   was disregarded by the board

      C   was initially done by the wrong people

9   The report found that those who actually carry out human resource accounting

      A   tend to use the same measurement criteria

      B   find the measurement procedures too rigid

      C   feel some things are too complex to measure

10   Katrin thinks that, in future, companies will be slow to measure their human resources because

      A   they will not know how to apply the information they obtain

      B   management will see the process as being too expensive

      C   they will feel uncomfortable attributing a value to their staff

11   What is Katrin's general impression of the research report?

      A   it makes very specific conclusions about human resource accounting

      B   it suggests some interesting areas for further investigation

      C   it highlights disagreement about the approach to human resource accounting

Part 3

Questions 12 – 20

You will hear the CEO of a property company called AirBase talking about his attempt to turn around the failing company.

For questions 12 – 20, complete the sentences using no more than three words.

You will hear the recording twice.

The Turnaround of AirBase

The background

Over the past decade AirBase has raised funds that exceed its (12) .... and bought five airports and assorted other properties.

In the past 48 months the company has had (13) .... of more than £73 million.

Last year the group raised additional funds to repay (14) .... with an interest rate of 28%.

The 12-month plan

In the first six months any additional (15) .... is stopped and any inessential assets are sold.

By the third quarter all (16) .... should be in place along with a platform from which to build the company.

The achievements after 6 months

The cost of leasing the (17) .... has been reduced.

An overambitious building project that failed to get (18) .... has been halted.

The future

A Border Inspection Post will allow cargo such as (19) .... to be shipped through one airport.

Negotiations to sell some property used for (20) .... purposes are about to be completed.

Part 4

TASK ONE – THE REASON FOR OUTSOURCING THEIR FINANCIAL DIRECTOR ROLE

For questions 21 – 25, choose from the list A – F the comment each speaker gives for outsourcing the FD role.

TASK TWO – AN UNEXPECTED BENEFIT OF OUTSOURCING THAT ROLE

For questions 26 – 30, choose from the list A – F the unexpected benefit each speaker mentions about outsourcing the FD role.

You will hear the recording twice. While you listen you must complete both tasks.

A	to allow the other directors to focus on growth	Speaker 1.... (21)	**A**	achieving the best return when selling the company	Speaker 1.... (26)
B	to oversee the restructing of the finance team	Speaker 2.... (22)	**B**	improving communications with their bank	Speaker 2.... (27)
C	to increase the company's profitability	Speaker 3.... (23)	**C**	finding a full-time member of staff	Speaker 3.... (28)
D	to improve the quality of the management accounts	Speaker 4.... (24)	**D**	improving sales forecasting	Speaker 4.... (29)
E	to discover the profitable parts of the company	Speaker 5.... (25)	**E**	finding an alternative form of financing	Speaker 5.... (30)
F	to assist with a management take over		**F**	overcoming problems with a client	

271

Listening Mock Test Answer Sheet

Part 1

1

2

3

4

5

6

Part 2

7

8

9

10

11

Part 3

12

13

14

15

16

17

18

19

20

Part 4

21

22

23

24

25

26

27

28

29

30

Copyright information:

Part 1

Extract one - JIEB exam paper/ Liquidations Mon 10 Dec 2007

Extract two –from The Bottom Line – BBC Radio 4 – 7 July 2007

Extract three –from The Bottom Line – BBC Radio 4 – 3 March 2007

Part 2

From an ACCA research report – RR83 – Valuing Human Resources – Shraddha Verma and Philip Dewe, 2004

Part 3

From www.growthbusiness.co.uk case studies – Turnaround from Hell – 1 September 2004

Part 4

From www.myfd.co.uk five different case-studies - The non-executive director's view /Building a professional team in a dynamic young business / Building team confidence / Digital Rum / Resonance Instruments

Speaking Mock Test

TIME The test lasts 16 minutes

The test includes the following components:

Interview	2 minutes
Long turn	7 minutes
Collaborative task	4 minutes
Discussion	3 minutes

Part 1   2 minutes (3 minutes for groups of three)

Interlocutor

Good (morning/afternoon/evening). My name is …… and this is my colleague,……

And your names are?

Can I have your mark sheets, please?

Thank you.

First of all, we'd like to know a little about you.

Ask candidates the following questions in turn.

▶   Where are you both from?

▶   *(Candidate A)*, are you working or are you a student?

▶   And what about you, *(Candidate B)*?

▶   *(Candidate A)*, tell us something about your job / the course you are studying.

▶   And *(Candidate B)*, tell us about your job / the course you are studying.

Ask each candidate one further question, as appropriate.

▶   Could you tell us about something you find really interesting in your work/studies?

▶   What do you hope to be doing in your work 10 years from now?

▶   What was the main reason you decided to go into your particular area of work/study?

Thank you.

Interlocutor

Now, in this part of the test I'm going to give each of you a choice of two different topics. I'd like you to choose one of the topics and give a short talk on it for about a minute.

(Candidate A), it's your turn first. Here are your topics and some ideas to help you.

*Place **Part 2** booklets, open at the task, in front of each candidate.*

You have a minute to choose your topic and prepare your talk. After you have finished your talk, your partner will ask you a brief question about it.

    Up to one minute of preparation time

All right? Now, *(Candidate A)*, which topic have you chosen?

Candidate A

States chosen topic

Interlocutor

(Candidate B), please listen carefully to *(Candidate A's)* talk, and then ask him/her a brief question about it. *(Candidate A)*, would you like to start?

Candidate A

🕐   *One minute*

Interlocutor

Thank you. Now (*Candidate B*), can you ask (*Candidate A*) a question about his/her talk?

Candidates

🕐   *Up to one minute*

Retrieve booklets. Now select a different pair of tasks for Candidate B.

Interlocutor

Thank you. Now, *(Candidate B)*, it's your turn. Here are your topics and some ideas to help you.

*Place **Part 2** booklets, open at the task, in front of each candidate.*

You have a minute to choose your topic and prepare your talk. After you have finished your talk, your partner will ask you a brief question about it.

🕐   *Up to one minute of preparation time*

All right? Now, *(Candidate B)*, which topic have you chosen?

Candidate B

States chosen topic

Interlocutor

(Candidate A), please listen carefully to *(Candidate B's)* talk, and then ask him/her a brief question about it. *(Candidate B)*, would you like to start?

Candidate B

🕐   *One minute*

Interlocutor

Thank you. Now *(Candidate A)*, can you ask *(Candidate B)* a question about his/her talk?

Candidates

🕐   *Up to one minute*

Interlocutor

Thank you.

Part 2

Tasks for Candidate A

Debt

- ▶ the debts companies have
- ▶ how debts can become a problem
- ▶ things a company can do about its debts

Outsourcing financial services

- ▶ which services are outsourced
- ▶ why outsourcing is used
- ▶ the future of outsourcing

Tasks for Candidate B

IT Skills

- ▶ the core IT skills needed in accountancy
- ▶ the impact of IT on accountancy
- ▶ how accountants keep up with developments in IT

Business strategy and planning

- ▶ the need for a business strategy
- ▶ who is affected by a company's business strategy
- ▶ the best ways to explain the strategy

Takeover bid

Part 3

Interlocutor

Now, in this part of the test I'd like you to talk to each other. I'm going to describe a situation to you.

*Place **Part 3** booklet, in front of the candidates.*

A medium sized company in the service sector is considering making a takeover bid for a rival company. You have been asked to consider the performance and position of the target comapny. Discuss the type of information you need to collect about the company and where this might be available.

There are some discussion points to help you.

You have about three (four) minutes to discuss this.

Candidates

    Approximately five seconds

Interlocutor

Please start your discussion now.

Candidates

    Approximately three minutes (four minutes for groups of three)

Interlocutor

Thank you. (Can I have the booklet, please?)

Retrieve booklet.

Part 4

Interlocutor

Select any of the following questions as appropriate.

▶ What non-financial information may be relevant to the takeover bid?

▶ Why might the company decide not to make the bid?

▶ Why might a takeover be beneficial to the company?

▶ What financial implications would a successful bid have for the company?

Thank you. That is the end of the test.

Takeover bid

A medium-sized company in the service sector is considering making a takeover bid for a rival company. You have been asked to consider the performance and position of the target company. Discuss the type of information you need to collect about the company and where this might be available.

Discussion points:

▶ sources of financial information about the company

▶ how the performance of the company can be measured

▶ the reliability of information published in external reports

Reading Mock Test

Answers

Reading Mock Test Answers

Parts 1A and 1B

			Comments
0	**A**	known	Note that 'B' and 'D' do not fit grammatically
1	**D**	concerns	Although the meanings of 'applies' (B) and 'relates' (C) fit, they both require the following preposition 'to' and so should not be selected.
2	**A**	composed	C makes no sense while B and D are used primarily in relation to physical objects.
3	**B**	include	'Consist' must be followed by 'of', while A and D do not make sense.
4	**C**	value	'Worth' could also fit here, but 'value' is more appropriate.
5	**C**	rather than	'Except for' (B) and the other options clearly do not work in terms of the context, which can be understood by making sure that you read the entire sentence. Try out each option in it if you are not sure.
6	**A**	create	This is the only option that makes sense.
7	**B**	increase	Costs 'increase' rather than extend, develop or advance.
8	**D**	follows	Aside from the sense of the phrase, note that in order for each of the other options to be correct, a preposition is needed following the verb: arises FROM (A), 'results IN' (B), and 'relates TO' (C). Only 'follows' (D) can fit as a single word.
9	**D**	state	It is a common phrase that terms 'state' something.
10	**A**	consecutive	When talking about an unbroken period of days, the fixed phrase is 'on <u>consecutive</u> days'.
11	**C**	liable	None of the other options fits grammatically.
12	**B**	reflect	Note that in order for options A or D to be correct, a preposition is needed ('comply WITH' (A) and 'abide BY' (D)).

Part 2

		Comments
0	BY	This sentence needs a preposition and the only one that fits is 'by' since 'to be fuelled by' is a fixed phrase.
13	FOR	Again a preposition is needed and 'demand FOR' fits.
14	IS	You need to read forward in this sentence to see that it is in the present tense ('employers are'). 'Rising' is a present participle, 'number' is a singular noun so the only possible word is 'is'.
15	OF	'To take advantage of' is a fixed phrase.
16	THEIR	The possessive pronoun is referring back to 'organizations and professional bodies' so it must be 'their'.
17	OVER	You may originally have considered 'more than', or even 'fewer than', here but of course you are only looking for one word. You may have considered 'all' but the company only works with 90 out of the 100 FTSE 100 companies so that does not fit the sense. The only word that does fit the rubric and the sense therefore is 'over'.
18	INTO	We need a preposition here to go with 'insight' just as 'of' goes with 'understanding' in the immediately preceding phrase. You may have considered 'of' or 'in' or even 'for', but the only preposition that fits in the fixed phrase is 'into'.
19	US	The sentence actually makes sense as it stands but there is a missing word. The context dictates that, as the chairman is talking in the first person plural ('we'), the pronoun 'us' will fit.
20	AND	As the phrase before contains 'both' you should immediately look for the 'and' – which is the missing word here.
21	BOTH	You need to read the whole sentence carefully to realise that there are two linked ideas here. As in the previous question, the issue is 'both….and', except in this case it is 'both' that is missing.
22	AS	'As well' is a fixed phrase.
23	FROM/IN	Although 'to flow from' makes slightly better sense given the drift of the chairman's argument (he is looking for benefits over a period of time in the future, not just at one moment), 'to flow in' also makes sense and would be marked correct.
24	SUCH	The context shows that the chairman is giving examples of 'major expenditure', so the fixed phrase 'such as' is appropriate.

Part 3A and 3B

		Comments
0	MERGERS	In this list of nouns a plural noun is required.
25	COMPETITIVE	This is a word that it is very easy to misspell – remember that you drop the 'e' and add 'itive'. Correct spelling is essential in this Part.
26	EFFICIENCY	Grammatically a noun is needed so 'efficiency' is created.
27	CENTRAL	'One location' consists of an adjective and a noun, so clearly another adjective is required.
28	INCREASINGLY	The word 'more' would fit here, which is an adjective. To form a similar word from the verb/noun 'increase' you need to add two 'suffixes':'-ing' and 'ly'.
29	UNLIKELY	To write 'likely' here would not be to amend the given word at all, so this would have been marked wrong. In fact what was required by the surrounding context was a negative prefix, as often happens in this task.
30	REDUCTION	The preceding word 'a' makes it clear that a noun is required here.
31	ALLOCATION/ ALLOCATING	The preceding word 'the' makes it clear that a noun is required here.
32	SUCCESSOR	Again the context determines that a noun is required. Be careful about spelling: '–or' not '–er'.
33	PROPERLY	The surrounding context of 'may .... be brought' signifies that an adverb is required. These are often formed by adding 'ly' to an adjective as here.
34	ENTITLED	The context required a past participle of a verb, which typically end with '-ed'. Many candidates when this was set in May 2007 wrote 'titled', but in fact the correct form is 'entitled', that is a prefix 'en–' had to be added to 'titled'.
35	RESOLUTIONS	Although there may be occasions where both singular and plural nouns may be acceptable (as in Question 36), Question 35 clearly requires the plural form to agree with 'are'.
36	REQUIREMENT(S)	

		Comments
0	**B**	In the last sentence of B the quote from the Gulf company refers to 'missing crucial project deadlines' (delays) because of not being able to import skilled engineers etc (shortages of workers).
37	**C**	'Older people' in the statement relates to 'ageing … population' in the first sentence of paragraph C
38	**A**	You may have been tempted to pick D for this, but note that the statement refers to BOTH companies and workers. It is the very first sentence of paragraph A that makes this point.
39	**D**	The second sentence of paragraph D states how workers move to 'higher salary' jobs in the new country. This causes rising costs for the companies and relates back to the first sentence, which describes companies looking for 'cheap labour' getting 'caught out'.
40	**B**	The statement expresses more formally the meaning of the first three sentences of paragraph B, which refer to 'not a one-way trip', 'flights home' and 'returning'.
41	**A**	You can identify 'highly qualified' in the statement with 'well-educated' in paragraph A.
42	**C**	'Inside countries' in the statement relates to 'within national boundaries' in paragraph C.

Part 5

		Comments
0	**H**	Sentence H is always the one that fills the gap in this part of the exam.
43	**E**	If you look at the preceding and the following sentences, they both contain the word 'tax'. It is therefore reasonable to focus on E as the potential gap fill sentence since it also makes reference to a 'tax liability'. In addition, it refers to WIP. Finally, the meaning of sentence E – that tax bills will rise – fits in with the sense of the following sentence.
44	**C**	The first sentence in this paragraph mentions the importance of 'banking money faster' and sentence C mentions the importance of billing quickly, which is the change exhorted at the end of the first sentence.
45	**A**	The paragraph deals with 'managing expectations' and with charging agreed fixed amounts, so sentence A fits here.
46	**F**	The sentence following the gap gives the clue to selecting this sentence, since it refers to 'who is paying for what' ie invoices.
47	**B**	It is the last sentence of this paragraph that identifies sentence B as being the correct choice, referring to 'what you are billing them for'.
48	**G**	Again this sentence refers both backwards and forwards – backwards to the 'philosophy' of running practices as businesses, being more transparent and managing customers, and forwards to 'compliance' with regulation.

Part 6

		Comments
49	**B**	Sentence B paraphrases the end of the first paragraph's first sentence.
50	**C**	Sentence C reflects the sense of the last sentence in paragraph 2.
51	**D**	The second sentence of the third paragraph makes it clear that D is the correct answer here.
52	**A**	Sentence A expresses the meaning of 'cease processing the product' in the second sentence of paragraph 4.
53	**B**	The sense of the fifth paragraph is that it costs more money to make external sales than to transfer internally.
54	**D**	Sentence D echoes the meaning of the second sentence of the last paragraph.

Writing Mock Test

Answers

Question 1

Dear Ms Collinson

In response to your letter regarding the statutory audit of our client, CMD plc, I can provide the following information.

In January we upgraded our accounting package, and the improvements are described in the leaflet enclosed. This change should not present you with any significant difficulties.

Regarding the new assets we have used the historical cost convention and recorded them in the nominal ledger at acquisition cost. Depreciation has been charged monthly in line with the established accounting policy, taking residual values and useful economic lives into account.

Funding was a mix of debt finance from the bank, which took a fixed charge over the assets as security, and an equity share issue to a new shareholder.

We advised the client to implement the balanced scorecard as this has been shown to produce excellent results. During the year the client has found its new performance indicators easy to use and its business has improved as a consequence.

The period mentioned is convenient for your team to visit us and I look forward to offering them such information and assistance as they need.

Yours sincerely

187 words

Question 2

Report on credit policy and cash management

Further to your request for advice following recent events, we have pleasure in presenting certain matters for your urgent consideration.

Effective credit policy

To ensure good cash flow and prevent bad debts a credit policy must cover every stage of dealing with credit customers. It should incorporate credit checks and references, clear and enforced terms of credit including limits, prompt invoicing and banking, active monitoring and collection procedures, and recourse to legal measures when necessary.

Effects of bad debts

Two major bad debts together have severely depleted your working capital, and currently you cannot settle your immediate liabilities out of liquid assets. In addition your overdraft is approaching its limit at the bank. Finally as your customer base is reduced and orders have fallen, you have excess capacity.

Risks to your company

Cash shortages and reduced levels of business threaten your company's future as a going concern. Falling levels of business mean cash problems are more difficult to overcome, and the company may face insolvency.

Urgent steps to be taken

Immediate funding must be secured by negotiating with the bank. Replacement sources of revenue should also be sought by your sales team, but at the same time a rigorous credit policy must be put in place for both new and existing customers so the bad debt problem does not recur. You should consider reducing capacity and making cost savings.

We shall be happy to offer such further advice and assistance as you need in the future.

253 words

Listening Mock Test

Answers

Listening Mock Test Answers

Part 1

1	A
2	C
3	C
4	B
5	B
6	A

Part 2

7	A
8	C
9	C
10	B
11	C

Part 3

12	**(market) valuation**	'valuation' alone is an acceptable answer
13	**losses**	
14	**(mezzanine) finance**	'finance' alone is an acceptable answer
15	**spending**	
16	**management changes**	
17	**head office**	
18	**planning permission**	
19	**fresh produce**	
20	**residential**	

Part 4	
21	E
22	A
23	C
24	D
25	F
26	F
27	C
28	B
29	A
30	D

Speaking Mock Test

Answers

Suggested Answers to Speaking Mock Test

It is important to realise that there is no perfect answer to a speaking test in the way that there is to most exams and tests. Candidates could give a wide variety of answers to the same question and all be judged pefectly correct. We set out here some suggestions as to how the conversation could go were you to take the Mock Speaking test, but please appreciate that these are just suggestions and by no means a definite answer.

Part One

Where are you both from?

You could answer with the name of your college and city, eg AB University, Karachi

Are you working or are you a student?

Examples:

▶ I am currently working for the Local Government Finance Office in Madrid; or

▶ I am studying for the ACCA qualification with Green College.

Tell us something about the job/the course that you are studying:

I work in the credit control department, which is part of the accounts department of my company. I am responsible for contacting customers who have outstanding debts and arranging repayment schedules.

I am taking a course in accounting and business at my local university. I am in the final year and am studying optional modules in Risk Management and Financial Strategy. I hope to find a job as an analyst when I graduate.

Additional questions

What do you hope to be doing in your work 10 years from now?

I hope to have become a partner in the firm that I work for, possibly in one of the overseas offices, maybe the US.

Could you tell us something you find really interesting about your work/studies?

I really enjoy dealing with different business issues every day and solving problems. I enjoy using the theory of accountancy and applying it to a specific business.

I am fascinated by all aspects of taxation, and particularly enjoy the tax planning issues that come up in my syllabus. Taxation is an area of business that is relevant throughout the world.

What was the main reason you decided to go into your particular area of work/study?

I have always wanted to be an accountant as it opens so many doors and gives the opportunity to work in different parts of the world. I think that the work is always interesting and challenging.

Part Two

Debt

The debts companies have

▶ Debts to suppliers, locally and overseas: usually short term

▶ Debts to banks and other lenders: usually bigger and more long term

▶ Debts to leasing or hire purchase companies

▶ Debts to government departments, eg taxation, employee contributions

How debts can become a problem

▶ When not properly monitored and controlled

▶ When they have been not properly negotiated, eg interest rates are too high

▶ When they are not properly serviced, eg interest payments are not met

Things a company can do about its debts

▶ Negotiate with creditors to reschedule them

▶ Sell them to a factor, to gain a lower amount of cash immediately, rather than wait for payment

▶ Consult an insolvency practitioner to consider the options

Outsourcing financial services

Which services are outsourced (examples)

▶ Payroll

▶ Debt collection

▶ Credit control

▶ Legal services

Why outsourcing is used

▶ To eliminate wasteful resource being under-utilised

▶ To reduce costs

▶ To enable an expert to work on the particular area, eg a payroll expert

The future of outsourcing

▶ Likely to become more common (you can express your own views about this!)
▶ More useful for niche activities

IT skills

The core IT skills needed in accountancy

▶ Ability to manipulate financial data
▶ Spreadsheets
▶ Reports
▶ Ability to produce budgets and forecasts

The impact of IT on accountancy

▶ Has made routine and repetitive tasks easier
▶ Maybe we lose sight of the basics, ie the debits and credits?
▶ Speeds up tasks
▶ Reduces likelihood of human error

How accountants keep up with developments in IT

▶ Courses
▶ Professional journals
▶ Word of mouth
▶ Promotions by IT companies

Business strategy and planning

The need for a business strategy

▶ Enables a business to target its activities
▶ Enables a business to focus on core areas
▶ Can set realistic forecasts and projections
▶ Avoids less profitable or wasteful activities

Who is affected by a company's business strategy?

▶ More or less everybody!

▶ Directors and employees

▶ Stakeholders

▶ Customers and suppliers

The best ways to explain the strategy

▶ At company meetings

▶ Via internal employee communications

▶ Press releases, for example with end of year results

Parts 3 and 4

Takeover bid

Part 3

7 minutes (10 minutes for groups of three)

Interlocutor	Now, in this part of the test I'd like you to talk to each other. I'm going to describe a situation to you.
	A medium-sized company in the service sector is considering making a takeover bid for a rival company. You have been asked to consider the performance and position of the target company. Discuss the type of information you need to collect about the company and where this might be available.
	There are some discussion points to help you. You have about three (four) minutes to discuss this. (5 second pause). Please start your discussion now.
Discussion points	Takeover bid
	▶ sources of financial information about the company
	▶ how the performance of the company can be measured
	▶ the reliability of information published in external reports
Sample Discussion	A The place to start I suppose is the company's published financial statements, going back as far as possible.
	B We're not told whether the target is a listed company, but if it is then the information that's publicly available shouldn't be too out of date.
	A The recent balance sheets, income statements and cash flow statements will give us insights into the target's financial position and performance, and its ability to generate cash for future expansion…
	B …especially if we use ratio analysis, yes, but they won't tell us what its plans are in the future…
	A ….though in my experience you can get some idea of these plans from some of the narrative items published with the financial statements, such as the Chairman's report.
	B If it's listed we may be able to get hold of analysts' reports, and information on the share price going back years.
	A And the company's website will give us plenty of information about how it is structured and what it offers to customers.

Sample Discussion	B	Actually, press reports can be useful for that sort of thing too.
	A	But realistically we have to rely on the published financial statements for financial information until such time as we get to due dliligence etcetera.
	B	Yes, so we have to use the information in financial statements to measure and evaluate its performance, which means ratio analysis.
	A	I suppose the most useful measures will be of profitability and return, since these look at profits and earnings in the income statement, which is what we mean by the term 'performance'.
	B	Trends in gross and net margin are vital of course, and also trends in return on capital.
	A	We would want to compare them over time, true, but we would also want to make comparisons with those of similar companies, and also with the bidding company's figures.
	B	If the target's listed we'll be able to calculate the PE ratio and compare that with others' – it's always a very useful measure.
	A	If it's listed its financial statements will have been externally audited so we can be pretty well assured that the information contained in them is reliable…
	B	…not completely, naturally, but financial reporting and accounting standards certainly focus a great deal on the reliability of financial information, and a company of any size must comply with these.
Interlocutor		Thank you. Can I have the booklet back please?

Part 4

Interlocutor	What non-financial information may be relevant to the takeover bid?
Suggested response (A)	There is plenty of non-financial information that's relevant, such as the nature of the target's business, its employees and existing customers, its marketing, management and product.
Interlocutor	Why?
Suggested response (A)	Well, because a business comprises what it does rather than just a set of financial information.
Interlocutor	What do you think?
Suggested response (B)	I agree – and I think one of the key things is how well the bidder and the target's management get on. From what I've seen, what undermines most takeovers is disagreement and culture clash in the board room.
Interlocutor	Why?
Suggested response (B)	A takeover is a major change for both bidder and target company, and change is only a good thing if it is managed properly, so all the managers involved must be in agreement and work together to make the takeover successful.
Interlocutor	Why might the company decide not to make the bid?
Suggested response (B)	Most likely because the projected financial benefits are not sufficient to make it a worthwhile investment.
Interlocutor	Why?
Suggested response (B)	Well, ideally an investment should have a positive net present value if it's to be of value to the bidding company's shareholders.
Interlocutor	Do you agree?
Suggested response (A)	To an extent, but I think deciding not to make the bid may come down to operational or cultural issues – the company may conclude that running the combined business will be too complicated, or the differences between how the companies operate will be too great.
Interlocutor	Why might a takeover be beneficial to the company?
Suggested response (A)	Financially, if it's an investment that has a high return or pays back quickly then shareholder value will increase and the company will benefit.

Interlocutor	How about you?
Suggested response (B)	There may be operational benefits that only partly show up in financial results at first, like streamlined staffing, improved marketing and better processes.
Interlocutor	What financial implications would a successful bid have for the company?
Suggested response (B)	I think the key implications would derive from how the takeover was funded. If it meant taking on a lot of new debt then the company would be quite exposed if there were interest rate rises or an economic downturn.
Interlocutor	What do you think?
Suggested response (A)	It depends how you define 'successful'. In one way a bid is successful if it goes through, so the target is actually taken over at the end of the day, but really it's only successful if it results in increased shareholder value for the company – in which case, the financial implications are good.
Interlocutor	Thank you. That is the end of the test.